Contents

About this Book

KEY TO SYMBOLS

✚ map reference to the maps found in the What to See section (see below)

✉ address or location

☎ telephone number

🕐 opening times

🍴 restaurant or café on premises or near by

🚆 nearest train station

🚌 nearest bus stop

✈ travel by air

⛴ ferry crossings and excursions by boat

ℹ tourist information

♿ facilities for visitors with disabilities

✋ admission charge

↔ other places of interest nearby

❓ other practical information

▶ indicates the page where you will find a fuller description

This book is divided into five sections to cover the most important aspects of your visit to Malaysia.

Viewing Malaysia pages 5–14
An introduction to Malaysia by the author
    Malaysia's Features
    Essence of Malaysia
    The Shaping of Malaysia
    Peace and Quiet
    Malaysia's Famous

Top Ten pages 15–26
The author's choice of the Top Ten places to visit in Malaysia, with practical information

What to See pages 27–90
Places to visit Malaysia, with practical information highlighting:

    What to see in Peninsular Malaysia
    What to see in Sabah
    What to see in Sarawak
    3 suggested walks and 1 suggested tour
    Quick tips and food & drink

Where To... pages 91–116
Detailed listings of the best places to eat, stay, shop, take the children and be entertained.

Practical Matters pages 117–124
A visual section containing essential travel information.

Maps
All map references are to the maps found in the What to See section of this guide. For example, Kuching has the reference ✚ 82A1 – indicating the page on which the map is located and the grid square in which the city is to be found. A list of the maps in this travel guide can be found under 'M' in the index.

Prices
Where appropriate, an indication of the cost of an establishment is given by **$** signs:
$$$** denotes higher prices, **$$** denotes average prices, while **$ denotes lower charges.

Star Ratings
Most of the places described in this book have been given a rating:

😊😊😊   Do not miss
😊😊   Highly recommended
😊   Worth seeing

Essential
Malaysia

by Neil Wilson

Neil Wilson is an experienced travel writer
and photographer based in Edinburgh. He
has traveled widely in Europe, North Africa,
North America, Mexico, the Far East, and
Australia, and has written and photographed
more than 20 guide books for various
publishers, as well as contributing articles
to magazines and newspapers.

Above: *Residents of Bajau stilt village, Semporna*

AA Publishing

*Traditionally dressed
Chinese figurine*

Written by Neil Wilson

Edited, designed and produced by AA Publishing and
Periplus Editions. © Automobile Association
Developments Ltd 1998, 2001
Maps © Periplus Editions 2001
Reprinted May 1998; Reprinted April 1999
Reprinted 2001. Information verified and updated.

Distributed in the United Kingdom by AA Publishing,
Norfolk House, Priestley Road, Basingstoke,
Hampshire, RG24 9NY.

A CIP catalog record for this book is available from the
British Library.

ISBN 0 7495 1631 3

Published by AA Publishing, a trading name of Automobile
Association Developments Limited, whose registered
office is Norfolk House, Priestley Road, Basingstoke,
Hampshire, RG24 9NY. Registered number 1878835.

Color separation: BTB Digital Imaging, Whitchurch,
Hampshire.
Printed and bound in Italy by Printer Trento Srl

Find out more about
AA Publishing and the
wide range of services
the AA provides by
visiting our Web site at
www.theAA.com

Viewing
Malaysia

Above: *Chinese mansion in Georgetown*
Right: *traditionally dressed Chinese figurine*

Neil Wilson's Malaysia

A driver takes a brief rest in his trishaw in Kota Bharu

Muslim Malaysia
Islam was introduced to Malaysia by Muslim Indian traders in the 12th and 13th centuries, and has been the dominant force in the shaping of Malay culture. It is the official religion of the Malay majority. But the government maintains a multi-faith policy, so that mosques, temples and churches often share the same landscape.

An enduring feature of major Malaysian public holidays is the phenomenon known as *balik kampung*. Meaning "back to the village," it describes the great exodus of city-dwellers as they head off to the countryside to visit family and friends, and spend a few days delighting in the simple pleasures of *kampung* life: fresh air, tasty food, and the renewal of communal ties.

It is a good metaphor for Malaysia, an increasingly urbanized country that still manages to keep in touch with its rural roots. Malaysia is a young and ambitious nation – the government's long-term plan, called Vision 2020, is to see Malaysia attain the status of a fully developed country by the year 2020. But among the skyscrapers of Kuala Lumpur, Johor Bahru and Georgetown, you can still find that keystone of Malaysian life, the open-air market, where office workers shop for fresh country vegetables and the latest music CDs, and the savory smells of grilled *satay* and stir-fried noodles waft from the nearby hawker stands. At weekends the same city-dwellers like nothing better than to head for the nearest beach, lake or waterfall for a cooling swim and a picnic; the more adventurous set off for a hike in the forest.

For visitors, much of Malaysia's appeal lies in this combination of city and nature, where you can enjoy top quality hotels, restaurants and shopping along with the delights of beautiful beaches, lush rainforest, exotic wildlife, and spectacular coral islands.

Right: color and bustle in Kota Bharu central market

Malaysia's Features

Geography

• Area: 329,758sq km (Peninsular Malaysia 131,689sq km; Sabah 73,620sq km; Sarawak 124,449sq km). East Malaysia and Peninsular Malaysia are separated by the South China Sea: the distance between Kuala Lumpur and Kota Kinabalu is about 1,600km.

• Highest peaks: Gunung Kinabalu (4,101m), Sabah; Gunung Tahan (2,187m), Pahang.

• Longest rivers: Sungai Rejang, Sarawak, 560km; Sungai Pahang, Pahang, 432km.

• Climate: equatorial. Hot, wet, and humid all year round.

A typically busy street in Georgetown, Penang

Temperatures average 25–30°C, with relative humidities of 82–86 percent. Average rainfall: 2,500mm annually. The northeast monsoon (Nov to Mar) and the southwest monsoon (Jun to Oct) bring more wind and rain to the east and west coasts of Peninsular Malaysia respectively. Sabah and Sarawak are wetter during the monsoon. The highlands are generally several degrees cooler.

People and Society

• Population: 21 million (62 percent Malay, 29 percent Chinese, 8 percent Indian, 1 percent other).

• Religion: Muslim, Buddhist, Hindu, Christian, other.

• Languages: official language is Malay (Bahasa Malaysia, or BM), but English is widely spoken. Other languages include Chinese (Mandarin, Cantonese, Hokkien, Hainan, Teochew), Tamil, Telegu, Punjabi, Hindi, Gujerati, Urdu, and numerous native dialects.

• Economy: manufacturing, palm oil, natural gas, petroleum, timber, rubber.

Government

Malaysia's government is a federal constitutional monarchy with two legislative houses, the Senato and the House of Representatives. There are 11 states in Peninsular Malaysia (Johor, Kedah, Kelantan, Melaka, Negeri Sembilan, Pahang, Perak, Perlis, Pulau Pinang, Selangor and Terengganu), plus the federal territory of Kuala Lumpur; and two states in East Malaysia (Sabah and Sarawak), plus the federal territory of Labuan. The government is led by the Prime Minister, while the sultans of the peninsular states take turns acting as Head of State.

Essence of Malaysia

The attractions of Malaysia are many and varied, and if you have only a limited amount of time, you will need to be selective. If you are on a beach holiday, try to take in at least one city – either KL (Kuala Lumpur), Georgetown or Melaka. Don't miss the opportunity to walk through the rainforest and delight in the rich diversity of plants and wildlife, and to go snorkeling on a coral reef, and sample this magical undersea world at first hand.

Above: an exotic inhabitant of the Butterfly Farm, Penang

Above: shadow puppets in the National Museum, Kuala Lumpur

Right: a tranquil tropical idyll – the palm trees, deep blue sea and golden sands of Pulau Tioman

THE 10 ESSENTIALS

If you only have a short time to visit Malaysia, or you would like to get a good sampling of the country's numerous facets, here are the essentials:

• **Wander the streets** of KL, Melaka or Georgetown, and soak up the atmosphere of heritage and bustling commerce. Stop for a snack at a noodle stall.

• **Hire mask and fins** and go snorkeling on a coral reef. The variety of exotic marine life is breathtaking, from colorful corals, to the multitude of reef fishes.

• **Visit a Malay** *kampung* **(village) or a native longhouse (tribal communal dwelling)** for an insight into the everyday lives of rural communities, where grandparents tend to young children and folk gather for a chat.

• **Take a trip to one of Malaysia's hill resorts** (Bukit Fraser, Bukit Larut, Penang Hill), where you can escape the tropical heat while strolling in the gardens or admiring the views.

• **Take a walk through the rainforest** on one of the many hiking trails in Malaysia's national parks and local nature reserves.

• **Rub shoulders with the locals** amid the crowded stalls of a *pasar malam* (night market), and choose from the wide variety of snacks available.

• **Attend a cultural show** for a brief taste of the colorful dances and traditional ceremonies that play an important part in Malaysian culture.

• **Take a boat trip to a deserted beach**, and relax amid the classic Malaysian combination of soft, white coral sand, sparkling turquoise waters and emerald jungle fringed with coconut palms.

• **Eat dinner at dusk** in a traditional outdoor hawker center. Sample the traditional hawker dishes of satay, *nasi goreng*, curry *laksa*, *char kway teow* and Hainanese chicken rice.

• **Visit KL's Golden Triangle** to experience the modern Malaysia of soaring skyscrapers, vast shopping malls, designer boutiques and bars and nightclubs.

Above: *exploring the clear, blue waters off Sabah*

Top: *kite-flying, a popular rural pastime*

The Shaping of Malaysia

Above: *Alfonso de Albuquerque, the Portuguese invader who conquered Melaka*

40000–32000 BC
Paleolithic tool-makers inhabit Kota Tampan, Perak, and Niah Caves, Sarawak.

10000–3000 BC
Hoabinhian hunter-gatherers live on the peninsula, and are possible ancestors of some indigenous *Orang Asli* ('original people') groups.

4000–3000 BC
Austronesian people from Taiwan migrate to the peninsula and islands. These are likely to be ancestors of some of the peninsula's *Orang Asli*, as well as of Sabah and Sarawak's native people. Malays migrate to the peninsula from Indonesia and Thailand.

7000–500 BC
Hindu and Buddhist port kingdoms are established. Trade with China and India commences.

7th–14th centuries AD
The Malay Peninsula comes under the Hindu Sumatra-based Srivijaya trading kingdom. Chinese traders begin visiting Borneo.

*c*1400
The Sumatran prince Parameswara founds the sultanate of Melaka.

15th century
Melaka develops into the most important commercial port in Southeast Asia, and becomes a center for the spread of Islam throughout the Malay Peninsula and the archipelago. The sultanate of Melaka expands over most of the Malay Peninsula and eastern Sumatra.

1511
Melaka falls to the Portuguese, but its influence declines without Muslim patronage. Muslim merchants move to Brunei, whose territory encompasses Sabah and Sarawak.

Early 17th century
Melaka and the Malay states are repeatedly attacked by the Sumatran state of Acheh.

1641
The Portuguese garrison at Melaka surrenders to the Dutch.

Late 17th century
Minangkabau and Bugis migrants from the Indonesian archipelago flock to the peninsula.

1786
Captain Francis Light acquires Penang as a base for the British East India Company.

1795
After Holland's defeat in the Anglo-Dutch war of 1781–83, the British take over Melaka and other Dutch possessions in the Far East.

1819
The British occupy Singapore and their influence in the Peninsula increases.

1826
Unification of Melaka, Penang and Singapore under British

administration as the Straits Settlements.

1842
The 'White Rajah' rule of Sarawak begins with James Brooke's successful suppression of rebellions in exchange for land.

1874
The Treaty of Pangkor marks the beginning of British political control in the Malay Peninsula.

1877
Sabah becomes British North Borneo.

Late 19th century
Tin draws Chinese migrants; Indians are attracted by business opportunities.

1896
Perak, Selangor, Negeri Sembilan and Pahang unite to form the Federated Malay States, with Kuala Lumpur as capital.

1914
Johor joins with Kedah, Perlis, Kelantan and Terengganu to form the Unfederated Malay States.

1941
Japanese invade the Malay Peninsula and, one year later, Borneo.

1946
Creation of the United Malays National Organisation (UMNO) to promote political interests of Malays. Sabah and Sarawak become British crown colonies.

1948
All peninsular states, except Singapore, are united in the Federation of Malaya.

1948–60
"The Emergency": Malaysian Communist Party insurgents, opposed to British rule, wage a guerilla war.

1957
Malaya achieves independence. The declaration is made at Dataran Merdeka in KL on 15 August. Tunku Abdul Rahman is the first Prime Minister.

1963
Singapore, Sarawak and Sabah join Malaya to form the Federation of Malaysia.

1965
Singapore is separated from Malaysia, and becomes an independent republic.

1981
Mahathir Mohammed, leader of UMNO, becomes prime minister.

1999
Dr. Mahathir is again voted in to power.

Below: *Britain's occupation of Singapore saw Britain take a foothold in peninsular politics.*

Peace & Quiet

The stone bungalows of the hill-stations were built in the Tudor tradition and used as administrative offices as well as resthouses. Recent buildings have also adopted this style, with varying degrees of success.

Hill Resorts

Malaysia's famous hill-stations are a legacy of the colonial era; here, British planters and administrators sought refuge from the tropical heat and humidity. Bukit Larut (Maxwell Hill, ➤ 47) and Bukit Bendera (Penang Hill, ➤ 62) were cleared in the 19th century to provide a retreat for officials living in Taiping and Georgetown respectively, and are still dotted with colonial bungalows surrounded by rose gardens and neatly trimmed lawns.

Bukit Fraser (Fraser's Hill), 100km northeast of Kuala Lumpur (➤ 40), and the Cameron Highlands (➤ 40) were not cleared until the 1920s. Both have cottages, gardens and golf courses, but the Cameron Highlands were also cultivated with extensive tea plantations and vegetable farms. Apart from the cooler climate, the main attractions of the hill resorts include walks and jungle-treks, bird-watching, golf, superb views, and

tasty cream teas in "Olde English" style hotels. The Genting Highlands resort near Kuala Lumpur (➤ 41) is a resolutely modern affair: a rash of concrete luxury hotels and theme parks built around the central attraction of Malaysia's only casino complex.

National Parks

Among Malaysia's main attractions are the vast, magnificent tropical rainforests, which cover more than half the land area. Unfortunately, logging, agriculture, rubber and oil palm estates, and rapid industrialization have taken their toll. However, many national parks have been created to protect fragile ecosystems and wildlife,

Left: *Pulau Tioman provides a luxurious setting for a range of isolated beach resorts*

while also allowing public access. The biggest is Taman Negara (➤ 26), covering an area of virgin forest six times the area of nearby Singapore. There are forest trails around the park headquarters, and the adventurous can attempt a nine-day trip to the summit of Gunung Tahan and back. Other spectacular national parks include Niah (➤ 88), Pulau Perhentian and Bako (➤ 87 and 88) in Sarawak; and Kinabalu (➤ 78) in Sabah.

Beaches and Coral Islands

Beautiful tropical beaches are one of the main reasons for Malaysia's popularity with tourists. The best beaches are on the east coast of Peninsular Malaysia, especially on the offshore islands like Pulau Tioman (➤ 66), Pulau Perhentian (➤ 56), Pulau Redang and the Johor Isles; on Pulau Langkawi and Pulau Pangkor (➤ 56) in the west; and in Sabah, in the Tunku Abdul Rahman and Turtle Islands national parks. The palm-fringed beaches are great for sunbathing, and the coral islands off the east coast for snorkeling and diving. The west coast mainland beaches and those on Pulau Pinang, though attractive, can be murky and polluted.

Diving
Malaysia's dive industry is well established, particularly in Sabah. Pulau Sipadan lies off the southeast coast of Sabah, and is a world-class dive destination. Tours, instruction and equipment are available at major towns and all dive sites.

Malaysia's Famous

Dr. Mahathir Mohamad

Malaysia's best-known political figure is the country's longest serving prime minister. Born the son of a teacher in Alor Setar in 1926, he worked as a doctor before entering politics and became prime minister in 1981 as the leader of UMNO (United Malays National Organisation). Mahathir-ism saw the birth of concepts such as Malaysia Inc. – the development of the country via business-government partnerships – and the Multimedia Supercorridor, an area set aside for the encouragement of technological achievements.

Tunku Abdul Rahman

The first prime minister of an independent Malaysia is remembered in street names in almost every Malaysian city. A British-educated lawyer, he was born in 1903 and became president of UMNO in 1951, before successfully leading the team that negotiated his country's independence. He served as prime minister from 1957 to 1970.

P. Ramlee

The most famous name in Malaysian music and film is undoubtedly P. Ramlee, who created a contemporary Malay music genre in the 1940s and built up the local film industry as well. The songwriter, musician, actor and director has streets and memorials named after him in Kuala Lumpur and Penang.

Lat

The work of Malaysia's most famous and best-loved artist

Tunku Abdul Rahman, being installed as the nation's first prime minister in 1957

can regularly be enjoyed in the pages of the national daily newspaper, the *New Straits Times*. The cartoonist, a national institution, is a shrewd commentator on the fads, failings and preoccupations of Malaysia's people and politicians. His keenly observed sketches neatly capture the contrasts between *kampung* and city life, and the many dilemmas of a traditional culture faced with explosive technological progress. Original Lat cartoons are collectors' items, and he has published several books of compilations.

Top Ten

Above: *Cameron Highlands*
Right: *Packing tea*

1
Kuala Lumpur

 42B2

MATIC (Malaysian Tourist Information Complex)

✉ 109 Jalan Ampang, 50540 Kuala Lumpur

☎ (03) 2164 3929

🕐 Daily 9–6

🍴 Restaurants serving Malaysian specialties ($$–$$$)

🚌 Bus 24, 34, 176 or 182 from Kota Raya (Jalan Cheng Lock)

♿ Few

✋ Free

❓ Live cultural performances (Tue, Thu, Sat and Sun at 3:30)

Kuala Lumpur's lively Chinatown district

Malaysia's vibrant capital retains a core of colonial elegance amid the chrome and glass of modern shopping malls and skyscrapers.

Capped by the world's tallest twin towers, Kuala Lumpur (or KL) is one of the fastest developing cities in the world, with vast amounts of money being invested in new office buildings, shopping centers, communications systems, and city rail transport systems.

But despite all this frantic activity, KL manages to hold on to much of its historic appeal (► 31–9). The green square of Dataran Merdeka ('Independence Square'), once the center of the old, colonial city, still preserves a certain tranquillity amid the hurly-burly of traffic and towering skyscrapers, a feeling heightened by the restrained elegance of the surrounding buildings: the Royal Selangor Club, St. Mary's Church, and the Moorish façade of the Sultan Abdul Samad building.

The history of the ethnic communities that contributed to KL's multicultural population is preserved in a number of 19th-century mosques and temples, in the streets of Chinatown and Little India, and in the exotic flavors of the city's cuisines. No visit would be complete without a meal of *satay*, *ayam goreng*, or *char kway teow* at one of the many open-air hawker centers.

The modern city's numerous attractions include bargain-hunting in the Golden Triangle's air-conditioned shopping malls, and strolling through the greenery of the lovely Lake Gardens.

2
Pulau Pinang (Penang)

Fascinating temples, historic buildings and great beaches make Penang one of Malaysia's most popular tourist destinations.

The island of Penang lies off the west coast of Malaysia, at the northern end of the Straits of Melaka (➤ 57). It was acquired in 1786 by Captain Francis Light as a base for the East India Company, and thus became the British Empire's first foothold in the Far East. Captain Light built a stronghold at Fort Cornwallis on the easternmost point of the island, and supposedly encouraged workers to clear the surrounding forest by firing a cannon-load of coins into the bush. The newly established city of Georgetown boomed for a few decades. Chinese traders flocked there and made their fortunes from tin, rubber and copra, building opulent mansions along "Millionaire's Row" (Jalan Sultan Ahmad Shah). However, the city's development was eclipsed by the rising importance of its southern counterpart, Singapore, which was founded by Sir Thomas Stamford Raffles in 1819.

Georgetown is a large, modern city, but it has retained a fascinating historical core with a strong Chinese character that KL and Singapore have largely lost. Relics of the city's colonial past include some of the crumbling remains of Fort Cornwallis, the fine buildings around the Padang, the lush delights of the Botanical Gardens, and the cool retreat of Bukit Bendera (Penang Hill). Away from the city, the island's numerous attractions include its many fine beaches, fishing villages, jungle hiking trails and the incense-filled, colorful temples. Industry has been concentrated on the east coast between the harbor and the airport, while tourist development has taken place chiefly in Georgetown and along the north coast beaches at Batu Feringghi and Teluk Bahang.

✚ 42A4

Tourist Information Centre

✉ Komtar Shopping Centre, Jalan Penang, 10000 Georgetown. (There are also tourism offices at the airport and on Jalan Tun Syed Sheh Barakbah, behind Fort Cornwallis)

☎ (04) 261 4461

🕐 9:30 6

🚆 Railway station in Butterworth connects to Thailand and south to Singapore via KL

⛴ A 24-hour ferry service operates between Butterworth and Georgetown

❓ Penang is connected to the mainland by a 13.5km bridge. A toll is charged when crossing to the island, but not on the return trip

Colorful lanterns decorate the 19th-century temple of Kek Lok Si, Pulau Penang

17

3
Kinabalu National Park

 75B2

 100km northeast of Kota Kinabalu

 (088) 245742 (Kinabalu Gold Resorts, Kota Kinabalu)

 Daily, 24 hours

 Restaurants at park headquarters, and at Laban Rata on mountain ($)

 Bus or minibus from Kota Kinabalu to park entrance, 2-hour journey

None

Park entrance free; compulsory permit and guide for climbing mountain, moderate

Poring Hot Springs (➤ 77)

Mount Kinabalu's granite peak soars above the lush lower slopes

 Guided walks on nature trails. The climb to the summit (8.5km, 2,200m of ascent) takes two days and, though hard work, is within the capabilities of most fit and healthy hikers. (Not recommended for those with heart trouble or high blood pressure.) You will need walking boots, waterproofs, warm clothing (including gloves and hat), water bottle, trail food and a torch.

A mysterious world of lush forests, tree-ferns and pitcher plants surrounds the rugged granite pinnacles of Southeast Asia's highest mountain.

The 4,101m peak of Mount Kinabalu dominates the skyline east of Kota Kinabalu in Sabah. Its name derives from the belief of the local Kadazan people that the spirits of their ancestors inhabit the mountain: *aki nabalu* means 'revered place of the dead'. This huge mass of granite was injected

into the Earth's crust some nine million years ago; since then erosion has removed the softer surrounding rocks to leave the ice-sculpted summit dome projecting above the tree-line. Its slopes support a bewildering variety of plant communities, which change gradually with increasing height. The area was declared a national park in 1964. The park headquarters has a visitors' center, restaurants and accommodation. Hiking trails lead into the forest, ranging from one-hour strolls to the two-day ascent of Mount Kinabalu. The park's unusual flora includes almost 1,000 varieties of orchid, some growing in the Mountain Garden behind the visitors' center. Most famous are the insectivorous pitcher plants (*Nepenthes*), which trap insects in a water-filled leaf. The largest, *Nepenthes rajah*, has been found holding over two liters of water and a drowned rat!

4
Kuching

The former seat of the "white rajahs" overlooks the banks of the Sarawak River, and is an intriguing and easy-going blend of British and Bornean influences.

Kuching was founded in 1839 as part of the Brunei sultanate and came under the control of the British adventurer James Brooke in return for his assistance in quelling a tribal uprising. Brooke declared himself Rajah of Sarawak, but the town's "golden age" came during the reign of his nephew and successor, Charles (1868–1917), who oversaw the building of a palace (the Istana) for himself and his wife, Ranee Margaret (1870); a Court House (1874); Fort Margherita and the Square Tower (1879); and the grand Sarawak Museum (1891). Charles' eldest son, Vyner Brooke, was the last of the white rajahs (1917–46); Sarawak was taken by the Japanese in 1941, and became a British Crown Colony after the war, before joining the Federation of Malaysia in 1963. Kuching is an attractive mixture of the old and the new (➤ 84–6). The waterfront overlooks the swirling brown waters of Sarawak River, and is a pleasant place to stroll, with views across the broad river to Fort Margherita and the Istana. Behind the waterfront there is a lively Chinatown, with several fascinating antique shops and some excellent food stands. The green square of the Padang was the heart of the 19th-century city, and is still bordered by the elegant façades of the Court House, the Post Office and the famous Sarawak Museum, which is one of the best museums in Southeast Asia. Kuching is also a good center from which to explore southwestern Sarawak. Local travel agents can arrange river safaris, which include visits to Iban longhouses in the interior, or trips to the national parks of Semenggok, Bako, and Gunung Gading.

✚ 82A1

Visitors' Information Centre Kuching

✉ 31 Jalan Masjid, 93400 Kuching

☎ (082) 410944

🕐 Mon–Thu 8–4:30, Fri 8–4:45, Sat 8–1 Closed Sun

🍴 Nearby ($)

♿ None

✋ Free

A stall-holder points out a bargain at Kuching's Jalan Satok market

5
Pulau Langkawi

42A5

Tourist Information Centre

 Jalan Persiaran Putra, 07000 Kuah

 (04) 966 7789

Daily 9–1, 2–6

Express ferries to Pulau Langkawi run every 90 minutes between 8 and 6 from Kuala Kedah (a one-hour journey), hourly from Kuala Perlis (a 40-minute journey), and once a day from Penang (a 2½-hour journey)

Daily MAS flights to Langkawi from Kuala Lumpur, Penang and Alor Setar (☎ 03 746 000). Air Asia also services Langkawi (☎ 03 745 7777)

Cars, motorcycles and bicycles can be hired at the Kuah jetty and at Pantai Cenang and Pantai Tengah.
Boats for island-hopping (4 hours) can be booked at Tanjung Rhu, Pantai Cenang and Kuah. The Langkawi Yacht Club at Kuah offers sunset cruises

Once the haunt of fishermen and pirates, Pulau Langkawi now attracts tourists with its white, sandy beaches, limestone peaks, and waterfalls.

Pulau Langkawi lies 30km off northwestern Malaysia, surrounded by more than 100 mainly uninhabited islands. The island is 30km long and 16km wide. It has an international airport, accommodations ranging from luxurious resorts to backpackers' hostels, golf courses, and attractions based on the island's many legends. The main town of Kuah is small but busy, with shopping centers taking advantage of the island's duty-free status. The main focus for tourists is the beach strip of Pantai Cenang and Pantai Tengah on the west coast, which is lined with restaurants and hotels. There are also good beaches at Pantai Kok, Tanjung Rhu, and Datai.

Less than an hour's walk from Pantai Kok is the waterfall of Telaga Tujuh (Seven Wells), where a stream cascades 100m during the rainy season. There are other scenic waterfalls at Temurun, near Datai, and Durian Perangin, 15km north of Kuah. Coral-fringed islands dot the

Right: the spectacular Telaga Tujuh waterfall

coastal waters. Boat trips visit Pulau Dayang Bunting, with its freshwater lake, and the wildlife sanctuary of Pulau Singa Besar. Pulau Payar, 30km south, is a marine park where you can dive, snorkel or view the coral reef from glass-bottomed boats.

Above: *discovering the beautiful Langkawi archipelago by boat*

6
Taman Negara

43C3

Park headquarters reached via a 59-km riverboat trip from the jetty at Kuala Tembeling (a 4-hour drive from Kuala Lumpur). Kuala Tembeling can also be reached by train from Kota Bharu, Johor Bahru and Singapore

(03) 9075 2872 (Dept of Wildlife and National Parks, Kuala Lumpur); (03) 2164 3929 (Taman Negara Resort); (09) 266 2369 (Nusa Camp)

Restaurants attached to resorts, and in the village near park HQ ($–$$$)

Permits for entry, fishing and photography: inexpensive
Accommodation and boat: inexpensive to expensive
Tour guides compulsory for Gunung Tahan climb

Organized tours from Kuala Lumpur

Water buffalo in Taman Negara

The green heart of Peninsular Malaysia is a treasure-trove of rainforest plants and a sanctuary for a great variety of wildlife.

Taman Negara (the name simply means 'national park') encompasses 4,343sq km of tropical rainforest, an area more than six times the size of Singapore. Established in 1938 (when it was called the King George V National Park), it lies on the north side of the Tembeling River and includes Gunung Tahan (2,187m), the highest summit in Peninsular Malaysia.

A diverse range of habitats and plant communities exists within the park boundaries. The dense, evergreen forests of the lowlands are characterized by tall tropical hardwoods draped in thick, creeping lianas, and the more open montane forests of oak, laurel and native conifers. In contrast, the slopes of the high-level (above 1,500m) cloud forests of Gunung Tahan support a bizarre growth of gnarled rhododendrons, giant heather, tree-ferns, as well as dwarf oaks draped in mosses, ferns, orchids and pitcher plants.

Don't expect to see rare species such as tiger, leopard, sun bear, rhinoceros or elephant on a flying visit. A night spent at one of the park hides, overlooking a salt-lick, can result in an encounter with wild ox, wild boar, tapir, and various species of deer, however. Primates such as macaques, leaf monkeys and gibbons are more often heard than seen in the dense vegetation. More easily seen – but be sure to bring binoculars and telephoto lens – are the 250 species of birds that inhabit the park, including spectacular varieties such as the giant argus pheasant, hornbills, trogons, pittas, kingfishers, and eagles. A network of hiking trails radiates from the park's headquarters to various camps, hides, caves and peaks. Treks range in duration from a few hours to a nine-day round-trip to the summit of Gunung Tahan.

7
Pulau Perhentian

Clear, turquoise waters, gently waving palm trees and soft sands make Perhentian the quintessential tropical island paradise.

Backpackers brought tourism to the two Perhentian islands in the early 1990s in search of an alternative to over-developed destinations. Lying about 20km off the state of Terengganu in the northeast corner of the peninsula, the pair comprises Perhentian Besar and Perhentian Kecil (*besar* means big, *kecil* small). A traditional fishing enclave, the islands provided monsoonal refuge for 15th-century trading ships. The Perhentian are, for now, the least developed of Peninsular Malaysia's resort islands.

The old Malay wooden fishing village on Perhentian Kecil, with its brightly painted boats, is particularly picturesque at dusk. This is when the locals gather on the beachfront to chat. However, the perfect, white, powdery beaches lapped by crystal clear waters are the islands' biggest draw. The original backpacker stretch, Pasir Panjang (long beach) on the smaller island, has gone a little upmarket although rock-bottom basic accommodation is still available. Tiny village-style resorts and a few upmarket hotels now dot both islands.

The lovely waters are great for swimming and coral reefs just offshore provide great snorkeling. Scuba divers will find leisurely diving here among colorful, soft coral gardens, populated by darting reef fish. Dive instruction, tours and equipment are available. Sunsets are lovely from Coral Bay on Perhentian Kecil. Trails snake through the thick, hilly rainforest of both islands, offering the hiker many fantastic views. The islands are closed to visitors during the monsoon months of November–February.

A tranquil scene on Pulau Perhentian

 43C4

P.P.P.P.P. (Association of Perhentian Island Tour Operators)

 Jetty, Kuala Besut, 22300 Terengganu

 (09) 691 0320

🕐 7–5

🍴 Restaurants at resorts and chalets ($–$$)

⛴ Scheduled departures to the big resorts; services from 9–2. Crossing takes 1½ hours

❌ The nearest airports are Kota Bharu and Kuala Terengganu. Taxis and buses go to Kuala Besut

❓ More information is available from tourism offices in Kota Bharu and Kuala Terengganu

23

8
Melaka

43C1

Melaka Tourist Information Centre

Jalan Kota, 75000 Melaka

(06) 283 6538

Daily 9–4:30

Sound and Light Show nightly at 9:30, at the Padang. Admission charge

Open to the skies: the hilltop church of St. Paul's in Melaka

History lingers along the banks of the Melaka River, once the most important trading harbor in the Malay Archipelago.

In 1400 an exiled Sumatran prince, Parameswara, founded a town on the site of a *melaka* tree, where he had witnessed a mouse deer attack one of his hunting dogs. The town had a fine natural harbor on the main sea route between India and China, and it quickly developed into a prosperous commercial port frequented by Indian, Persian, Arabian and Chinese merchants. At its height, the Sultanate of Melaka controlled the whole Malay Peninsula and much of Sumatra, and was responsible for spreading Islam throughout the region.

But Melaka's wealth attracted the attention of Portuguese traders, and the city fell to Alfonso d'Albuquerque in 1511. It was taken by the Dutch in 1641, before finally passing into British control in the 1820s. With the silting of Melaka's harbor and the increasing importance of Singapore, the town gradually declined into a sleepy backwater, and remained that way until its rebirth as a tourist destination. Melaka's colorful trading past and its colonial masters have left their mark on the city's architecture, food, and people. Its long and cosmopolitan history makes it one of the most fascinating cities in Malaysia.

Melaka's attractions include the charming hilltop church of St. Paul's; the ruined 16th-century gateway to the Portuguese fort of A Famosa; the striking 17th-century Dutch Stadthuys (Town Hall); the interesting Melakan mosques with their distinctive, Sumatran-influenced architecture;

and the beautiful Peranakan town houses (➤ 49–52). Melaka is also famed for its crafts and antique shops, many of them clustered along Jonkers Street (now called Jalan Hang Jebat).

9
Cameron Highlands

Cradled among the mist–shrouded peaks of the peninsula's interior, this rural retreat offers a welcome respite from the tropical heat.

Sixty kilometers of steep, winding road lead from Tapah up to the cool and misty heights of the Cameron Highlands. This fertile fold in the forest-clad mountains of the Main Range, discovered in 1885 by the British surveyor William Cameron, lies 1,500m up, and has an average daily temperature of 22°C. It was developed as a hill station in the 1920s–'40s, with large tea-estates and small Chinese market-gardens. Today, planters' bungalows have been turned into inns, still surrounded by rose gardens. There are also newer hotels and a public golf course.

The main tourist center is Tanah Rata, whose main street is lined with cheap Chinese hotels, cafés, shops and hawker stands. Chalets, backpackers' hostels and more expensive hotels can be found on the fringes of town. About 2km north of Tanah Rata is the Smokehouse Hotel, a large mock-Tudor hotel built in 1937, which appears to have been transplanted straight from England, complete with oak-beam ceilings, log fires and a red telephone box.

A main attraction is walking or driving through a tea estate. The pretty Sungai Palas is on the road to Gunung Brinchang (Mount Brinchang), which, at 2,031m, is the highest peak in the Cameron Highlands. A viewing tower at the summit offers a superb panorama in clear weather. The Farlie tea estate at Habu, South of Tanah Rata, has the highland's oldest tea-processing factory. Both estates offer factory tours. The Cameron Highlands also has numerous marked hiking trails that go through farms and lush forest.

✚ 42B3

✉ 90km from Tapah, Perak

☎ (05) 491 2318 (Jade Holidays, Brinchang)
(05) 491 2073 (Wilderness Journeys, Brinchang)

🍴 Many restaurants and hawker stands in Tanah Rata and Brinchang ($–$$)

🚌 Regular bus service from Tapah, Ipoh and Kuala Lumpur

♿ None

❓ Half-day to several day tours, from farm visits to jungle trekking

The rolling green acres of a tea plantation in the Cameron Highlands

10
Niah National Park

83C2

110km south of Miri, Sarawak

(085) 436637 (National Parks Office, Miri); (085) 737450 (Niah National Park) Daily 8–4:30, Park HQ 8–5

Cafeteria at park HQ ($)

The awe-inspiring limestone caverns of Niah, their walls daubed with primitive paintings, have provided shelter for humans for 40,000 years.

Bones discovered in the Niah Caves in the 1950s prove that *Homo sapiens* was living here 40,000 years ago, the oldest evidence of human habitation yet found in Southeast Asia. The caves were first described to Europeans by the British naturalist Alfred Russel Wallace in 1864, but it was a century before the Sarawak museum

Bus (2 hours) from Miri and Bintulu to Batu Niah, then boat or taxi (5 minutes) to park HQ

None

Park entrance free; permit compulsory; boat and accommodation: moderate

Gunung Mulu National Park (➤ 88)

Organized tours from Kuching and Miri are available; book at the Visitors' Information Centre in either Miri or Kuching. Accommodation is also available in Batu Niah.

uncovered Stone Age tools and a man's skeleton dating from 38,000 BC. There were also cave paintings and "boat burials" (graves in which canoes were used as coffins) thought to be 1,000 to 2,000 years old.

Niah and the surrounding forest were made a national park in 1975, and some of the archeological findings are displayed at the park headquarters at Pangkalan Lubang. A raised boardwalk leads from the park headquarters to the caves, through rainforest where you can see macaques, hornbills, bulbuls, trogons and butterflies, and perhaps flying lizards, water monitors and mouse deer. The Great Cave at Niah is over 90m high and 180m wide, and is inhabited by millions of bats and swiftlets, whose twilight comings and goings are an impressive spectacle. The boardwalk continues into the darkness (bring a torch) and along a passage to the Painted Cave, where prehistoric paintings adorn the walls. Accommodations are available at park headquarters: book at the National Parks Office in Miri or Niah(➤ 88) or Kuching (➤ 19, 84–6).

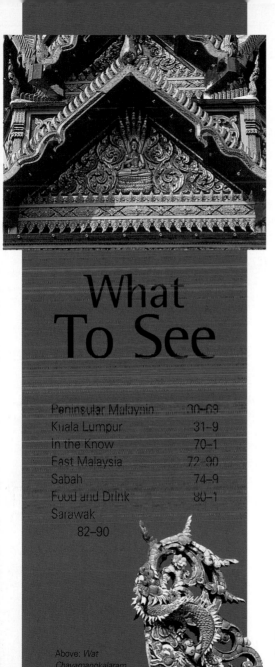

What To See

Above: *Wat Chayamangkalaram*
Right: *Khoo Kongsi, Georgetown*

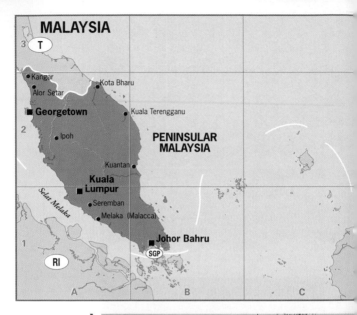

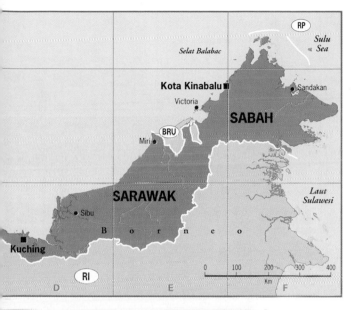

Boats moored up
in the waters off
Pulau Langkawi

29

Peninsular Malaysia

Malaysia is divided into two parts by the South China Sea. Peninsular Malaysia occupies the tip of the Southeast Asian mainland, while the two states of Sabah and Sarawak (East Malaysia) lie in the northern part of the island of Borneo. The more densely populated Peninsular Malaysia combines ultra-modern cities with historical pockets such as Kuala Lumpur and Georgetown, and idyllic rural scenery. Development is concentrated on the west coast, around the centuries-old trade shipping route through the Straits of Melaka. Today, excellent transport networks, including the North-South Highway, make traveling easy. Beyond the mighty Banjaran Tititwangsa mountain range is the east coast, heartland of traditional Malay culture. Here are superb beaches and offshore coral islands such as the Perhentian and Johor isles. A visit to Taman Negara reveals the delights of the rainforest-clad interior.

' I see it now – the wide sweep of the bay, the sands, the wealth of green infinite and varied, the sea blue like the sea of a dream... '

JOSEPH CONRAD
Youth (1902)

Kuala Lumpur

Kuala Lumpur is a sprawling city of 1.3 million people – the commercial, financial and political capital of modern Malaysia. First impressions are of gleaming skyscrapers, concrete freeways and countless building sites, but the city has managed to preserve many fascinating aspects of its history

Kuala Lumpur's Parliament House

Kuala Lumpur has come a long way since it was founded by Chinese tin prospectors in 1857. The miners' settlement at the meeting of the Klang and Gombak rivers (*'kuala lumpur'* means 'muddy confluence') grew rapidly in the 1880s following the construction of a railway link with the port of Klang, and its central location led to its selection in 1895 as the capital of the Federated Malay States. Grand colonial government buildings were raised on the west side of the river, while wealthy merchants and rubber planters built their mansions along Jalan Ampang on the east bank. Today, nationalistic events are held on the green field of the Padang, overlooked by the Moorish façade of the Sultan Abdul Samad Building and the mock-Tudor Royal Selangor Club, once symbols of colonial supremacy. Across the river lies KL's Chinatown, with its bustling street markets and colorful temples, and on the neck of land where the Klang and Gombak meet is the Masjid Jame (Friday Mosque), built in 1897.

The city's other main attractions include the Lake Gardens, the cultural collections of the National Museum, and the glitzy shopping malls of the Golden Triangle, crowned by the world's tallest twin towers (➤ 16) housing offices and a shopping center.

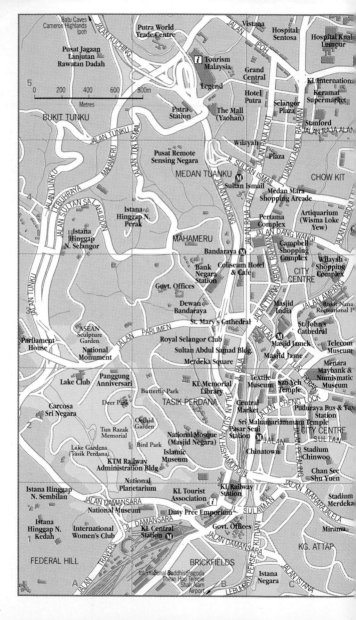

Batu Caves
Cameron Highlands
Ipoh

JALAN KUCHING

Putra World
Trade Centre

JALAN IPOH

Vistana

Hospital
Sentosa

Hospital Kuala
Lumpur

Pusat Jagaan
Lanjutan
Rawatan Dadah

i Tourism
Malaysia

Grand
Central

KL International

Legend

Hotel
Putra

Keramat
Supermarket

5

0   200   400   600   800m

Metres

Putra
Station

The Mall
(Yaohan)

Selangor
Plaza

Stanford

BUKIT TUNKU

JALAN TUNKU

JALAN RAJA LAUT

TUANKU ABDUL RAHMAN

JALAN RAJA ABDULLAH

Wilayah

Plaza

JALAN TUNKU

JALAN TUN ISMAIL

Pusat Remote
Sensing Negara

JL SULTAN ISMAIL

CHOW KIT

LEBUHRAYA

MAHAMERU

JALAN SULTAN SALAHUDDIN

MEDAN TUANKU

Sultan Ismail

Medan Mara
Shopping Arcade

Istana
Hinggap N.
Perak

JALAN KUCHING

Pertama
Complex

Artiquarium
(Wisma Loke
Yew)

Istana
Hinggap
N. Selangor

MAHAMERU

JALAN DANG WANGI

JALAN TUANKU ABDUL RAHMAN

Campbell
Shopping
Complex

Wilayah
Shopping
Complex

JALAN TUNKU

Bandaraya

Bank
Negara
Station

Coliseum Hotel
& Cafe

CITY
CENTRE

JALAN AMPANG

Govt. Offices

Dewan
Bandaraya

Masjid
India

Bukit Nana
Recreational P

St. John's
Cathedral

St. Mary's Cathedral

Parliament
House

ASEAN
Sculpture
Garden

JALAN PARLIMEN

Royal Selangor Club

Masjid Jamek

Telecom
Museum

National
Monument

Sultan Abdul Samad Bldg

Masjid Jame

Menara
Maybank &
Numismatic
Museum

Lake Club

Panggung
Anniversari

Merdeka Square

JALAN RAJA

KL Memorial
Library

Textile
Museum

Sze Yeh
Temple

JALAN BENTENG

JALAN CHENG LOCK

Carcosa
Sri Negara

Butterfly Park

TASIK PERDANA

Central
Market

Puduraya Bus & Tax
Station

Deer Park

Sri Mahamariamman Temple

CITY CENTRE
SULTAN

Tun Razak
Memorial

Orchid
Garden

National Mosque
(Masjid Negara)

Pasar Seni
Station

JALAN

JALAN SULTAN HISHAMUDDIN

Lake Gardens
(Tasik Perdana)

Bird Park

Islamic
Museum

Chinatown

Stadium
Chinwoo

JALAN PETALING

KTM Railway
Administration Bldg

Chan See
Shu Yuen

Istana Hinggap
N. Sembilan

National
Planetarium

KL Tourist
Association

KL Railway
Station

JALAN MAHARAJALELA

Stadium
Merdeka

JALAN DAMANSARA

National Museum

Duty Free Emporium

JL DAMANSARA

SULAIMAN

Mirama

Istana
Hinggap N.
Kedah

International
Women's Club

KL Central
Station

Govt. Offices

JALAN KUTAN

KG. ATTAP

JALAN DAMANSARA

LEBUHRAYA PERSEKUTUAN

JALAN ISTANA

FEDERAL HILL

JALAN TRAVERS

BRICKFIELDS

International Buddhist Pagoda
Thean Hou Temple
Shah Alam
Airport

Istana
Negara

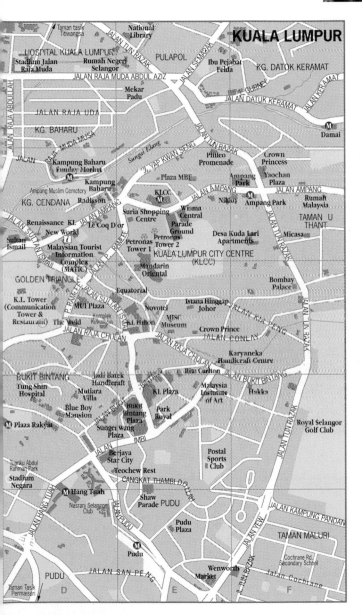

KUALA LUMPUR

What to See in the City Center

CENTRAL MARKET (PASAR SENI) ★★

+ 32C2
✉ Jalan Hang Kasturi
☎ (03) 2274 6542
🕐 Daily 10–10
🍴 Restaurants, food stands ($)
🚌 Bus terminal and LRT
↔ Chinatown, Dataran
   Merdeka (► below)

This Art Deco building on the east bank of the Klang river was built in the 1930s as the city's meat and vegetable market, but has since been converted to a lively collection of shops, restaurants and handicraft stands. It is connected by a walkway to the Dayabumi complex, across the river. Cultural shows are occasionally performed here.

CHINATOWN ★★★

+ 32C2
✉ Jalan Petaling
🍴 Hawker stands ($)
🚌 Near major bus terminals
♿ None
↔ Pasar Seni (► above)

Opposite page: *the Masjid Jame* Below: *a food stand in KL's Chinatown*

Although the Chinese population is now spread throughout the city, this district of ancient two-story shophouses east of Central Market retains the bustling commercial atmosphere of old KL, especially in the teeming *pasar malam* (night market) on Jalan Petaling, where the pavements are jammed with stands selling leather goods, watches, clothing, cassettes and CDs, souvenirs and bric-à-brac, and the aromas of Chinese cooking waft from the crowded stands and restaurants.

DATARAN MERDEKA (INDEPENDENCE SQUARE) ★★★

+ 32B3
✉ Jalan Raja
🍴 In the underground
   complex
♿ None
🎫 Free
↔ Masjid Jame (see below),
   Sultan Abdul Samad
   Building (► 37)

Formerly known as the Padang (Malay for 'field'), this wide expanse of vivid green turf marks the heart of old Kuala Lumpur. It is surrounded by reminders of the city's colonial past: the ornate Sultan Abdul Samad Building (► 37); the mock-Tudor premises of the Royal Selangor Club, focal point of KL's high society since the 1890s; the white spire of St. Mary's Cathedral, built in 1894; and the Memorial Library, housed in a grand old 1909 office building.

A plaque set in the turf marks the spot where the Union Jack flag was run down on 31 August 1957, as the country proclaimed its independence (*merdeka*). The Malaysian flag now flies here on one of the world's tallest flagpoles.

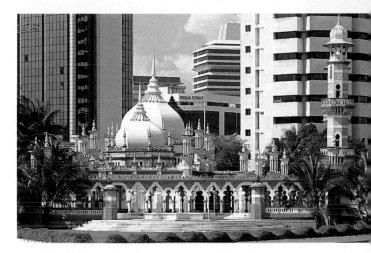

GOLDEN TRIANGLE & BUKIT BINTANG ✪✪✪

The Golden Triangle, east of the Klang river, is a glitzy district of high-rise offices, five-star hotels, upmarket shopping malls, nightclubs and restaurants. It is dominated by the twin steel-and-glass spires of the Petronas Towers, at 452m among the world's tallest buildings. The street that never sleeps, Bukit Bintang, the heart of the Golden Triangle's shopping district, is a shopper's paradise.

MASJID JAME (JAME MOSQUE) ✪✪✪

The prettiest of Kuala Lumpur's mosques was built in 1909 to the design of British architect A B Hubbock, who drew inspiration from the Mogul mosques of northern India. The building is a delicate confection of colonnades, onion domes and minarets, made of red-and-white brick and set on the neck of land at the confluence of the Klang and Gombak rivers.

MASJID NEGARA (NATIONAL MOSQUE) ✪

A 73m-tall minaret marks the site of Malaysia's National Mosque, a celebration of Islam in white marble with fountains set amid landscaped gardens. Built in the 1960s, the mosque can accommodate up to 8,000 worshippers beneath its 18-pointed umbrella dome (symbolizing the 13 states of Malaysia plus the Five Pillars of Islam).

MENARA KL (KL TOWER) ✪

This telecommunications tower sits atop Bukit Nanas overlooking the Golden Triangle (➤ above), and is a distinctive landmark. At 421m it is one of the tallest towers in the world, and the revolving restaurant and viewing galleries at the top provide a truly magnificent panorama of the city.

✚ 33D2–4, E2–4
✉ Jalan Sultan Ismail, between Jalan Ampang and Jalan Imbi
🍴 Hawker stands ($)
🚌 Buses from Bangkok Bank, Puduraya
Ⓔ LRT stations
↔ Menara KL (➤ below)

✚ 32C3
✉ Jalan Tun Perak
🕐 Open daily except prayer times
Ⓔ LRT Masjid Jame
🎟 Free
↔ Dataran Merdeka (➤ above)
❓ Dress suitably (➤ 70)

✚ 32B2
✉ Jalan Sultan Hishamuddin
🕐 Sat–Thu 9–6, Fri 2.45–6
🎟 Free
❓ Dress suitably (➤ 70); robes are provided for visitors wearing shorts or skirts

✚ 33D3
✉ Jalan Puncak
☎ (03) 208 5448
🕐 Daily 10–8
🍴 Seri Angkasa ($$$)
🎟 Moderate
↔ Golden Triangle (➤ above)

32A1
- ✉ Jalan Damansara
- ☎ (03) 282 6255
- ⏰ Daily 9–6
- 🚌 Buses from Pudu Raya
- ♿ Few
- ✋ Inexpensive (under 12s free)
- ↔ Taman Tasik Perdana (► 38)

32B2
- ✉ Jalan Sultan Hishamuddin
- 🍴 Restaurant and snack bars
- 🚆 KTM Komuter trains, LRT Pasar Seni
- ↔ Masjid Negara (► 35)

MUZIUM NEGARA (NATIONAL MUSEUM) ✪

The National Museum building dates from 1963, and reflects various aspects of traditional Malay architecture. Displays cover local history and culture, traditional arts and crafts, and Malaysian wildlife. Transport exhibits in the grounds around the museum include traditional boats, a Penang Hill funicular railway car, a Scottish-built aircraft, a fire engine, vintage cars, and one of the first Proton Saga cars to be built in Malaysia.

RAILWAY STATION ✪✪

Kuala Lumpur's main railway station, an architectural fantasy designed by A B Hubbock and built in 1910, is one of KL's most famous colonial landmarks. It is a magnificent concoction of Moorish spires and minarets, keyhole arches and cupolas, complemented by the equally ornate façade of the KTM Berhad (Malayan Railways) administration building across the road.

32C2
- ✉ Jalan Tun H. S. Lee
- ⏰ Early–late
- 🚌 Near major bus terminals
- 🚆 LRT from Pasar Seni
- ♿ None
- ✋ Free
- ↔ Chinatown (► 34)

For train passengers, KL's ornate railway station makes an impressive introduction to the city

SRI MAHAMARIAMMAN TEMPLE ✪✪✪

A back street in Chinatown harbors the magnificent *gopuram* of the Sri Mahamariamman Temple, a tiered gate tower of multi-colored ceramic tiles and ornate sculptures that surmounts the entrance to one of Malaysia's oldest Hindu temples. The temple was founded in 1873 on the site of the railway station, and was moved to this spot in 1885. It contains shrines devoted to the gods Shiva and Ganesh, and a silver chariot dedicated to the Lord Muruga that takes part in the annual procession from the temple to the Batu Caves (► 40) during the Thaipusam festival (► 116).

SULTAN ABDUL SAMAD BUILDING ✪✪

The Sultan Abdul Samad Building is one of KL's most familiar landmarks. The building, with its ornate Moorish façade of pink brickwork, white stucco, keyhole arches and copper-domed towers, was designed by the British architect A C Norman (who also designed St. Mary's Cathedral) in the 1890s, and was once the home of colonial government offices. It now houses the Malaysian Supreme Court and the High Courts.

✚ 32C3
✉ Jalan Raja
🕐 Not open to the public

Above: *intricate sculptures on Sri Mahamariamman Temple*

SZU YEH TEMPLE ✪✪

Tucked away down an alley is one of Kuala Lumpur's oldest Chinese temples, built in the 1880s. The construction of the tiny temple was completed with the aid of Yap Ah Loy, the first 'Kapitan China' (head of the Chinese community) in Kuala Lumpur. A century of incense smoke has darkened the red and gold decoration inside the temple, where a photograph of Yap Ah Loy can be seen on an altar near the back.

✚ 32C2
✉ Lorong Bandar, off Lebuh Pudu
🕐 Early–late
🚌 Near major bus terminals
🚻 None
💷 Free
🔄 Pasar Seni, Chinatown (► 34)

TAMAN BURUNG (BIRD PARK) ✪✪

A small, landscaped valley on the eastern edge of the Lake Gardens has been enclosed and stocked with a wide variety of Southeast Asian bird species. Footpaths and boardwalks lead among the forest glades and miniature waterfalls. A must for bird and nature lovers.

✚ 32B2
✉ Jalan Cenderawasih
🕐 Daily 9–5
🍴 Drinks and snacks
🚌 Tourist shuttle bus
💷 Inexpensive
🔄 Taman Orkid (► below)

TAMAN ORKID AND TAMAN BUNGA RAYA (ORCHID AND HIBISCUS GARDENS) ✪

Across the road from the Bird Park, set on a rounded hilltop, is KL's Orchid Garden. Over 800 species of Malaysian orchids are grown in the beds and pergolas laid out among ornamental ponds and walkways. A path at the far side leads into the neighboring Hibiscus Garden, which contains 500 varieties of Malaysia's national flower.

✚ 32B2/32A2
✉ Jalan Cenderawasih
🕐 Daily 9–6.30
🚌 Tourist shuttle bus
💷 Mon–Fri free; Sat–Sun inexpensive
🔄 Taman Burung (► above)
❓ Orchid Bazaar, weekends

32B2
Jalan Cenderasari
(03) 293 4799
Daily 9–5 (6 on weekends and holidays)
Restaurant
Moderate

TAMAN RAMA-RAMA (BUTTERFLY PARK) ✪✪

This enclosed garden contains over 100 species of colorful Malaysian butterflies, which can be seen at close quarters as they feed on trays spread with hibiscus blossom. The neighboring museum has displays of butterflies, moths, giant millipedes, scorpions and other exotic insects from all over Southeast Asia.

32A2
Main entrance on Jalan Parlimen; also accessible from National Mosque
Dawn–dusk
Hawker stands
Free
Muzium Negara (➤ 36), Masjid Negara (➤ 35)

TAMAN TASIK PERDANA (LAKE GARDENS) ✪✪✪

These 90-hectare gardens, set on wooded hills around an artificial lake, were laid out in the 1880s. The several kilometers of shady walks are popular with joggers and families. A deer park is home to the *kancil*, the local mousedeer, and there are orchid and hibiscus gardens. The National Planetarium and several museums line the road (Jalan Perdana) that winds towards the National Mosque.

Off map 32B1
Off Jalan Syed Putra
Daily 9–6
Hawker stands ($)
Free
? Lion dances and Chinese opera during Chinese New Year festivities

THEAN HOU TEMPLE ✪

On a hilltop a few kilometers south of the city center, this huge, modern temple is dedicated to the goddess of mercy, Kuan Yin, and is a popular venue for Chinese weddings. The temple and pagoda share the site with a 100-year-old Buddhist shrine and a sacred Bodhi tree.

Taman Tasik Perdana (Lake Gardens)

32A3
Off Jalan Parlimen (opp. the Lake Gardens)
Early till late
Drinks and snacks
Free
Taman Tasik Perdana (➤ 38)

TUGU KEBANGSAAN (NATIONAL MONUMENT) ✪✪

This large bronze sculpture commemorates the many soldiers who fought against the Communist insurgency in the 1950s during The Emergency. The sculpture pays tribute to Malaysian as well as British and other troops. Surrounding it is a sculpture garden honoring the 10-member ASEAN (Association of Southeast Asian Nations) economic grouping, of which Malaysia was a founding member.

A Walk Around Kuala Lumpur

This walk is a good introduction to many of Kuala Lumpur's main landmarks and includes a stroll through busy Chinatown. This district is fascinating for people-watching and informal street life.

From the LRT station visit the Masjid Jame (➤ 35), then head left along Jalan Tun Perak, beneath the raised LRT track.

Turn left into Jalan Raja at the colonnaded front of the old Dewan Bandaraya (City Hall). Walk along Jalan Raja.

This is KL's colonial core, with the impressive Sultan Abdul Samad building on your left and the Padang on your right, surrounded by other 19th-century buildings. These buildings are a unique mixture of Victorian architecture and Moorish elements and were designed by British architect A C Spooner.

Turn left at the Muzium Tekstil (Textile Museum) into Lebuh Pasar Besar and continue until Jalan Tun H S Lee. Turn right and take the left fork into Jalan Petaling (Petaling Street).

This is the bustling heart of Chinatown (➤ 34), where you can enjoy the general ambience of this colorful district and browse among the many stores and stands. The Chinese and Malay fast-food stands are authentic and inexpensive. In the evening, the street becomes a marvelous night market with brilliant lighting and authentic-looking copies of brand-name watches and clothing.

Two blocks down, turn right on Jalan Sultan, and right again along Jalan Tun HS Lee.

The walk now takes you past the impressive Sri Mahamariamman Temple (➤ 36).

Continue along Jalan Tun H S Lee, past Jalan Cheng Lock ,and turn left into Lebuh Pudu. The Sze Ya temple is on the left. The road leads to Pasar Seni (Central Market).

Join the bargain-hunters in Chinatown on your way around Kuala Lumpur

Distance
3km

Time
1 hour, excluding time spent visiting attractions

Start point
🔲 32C3
Masjid Jame LRT station

End point
Pasar Seni
(Central Market)
🔲 33C2

Lunch
Old China Café ($$)
✉ 11, Jalan Balai Polis
☎ (03) 232 5915

 42A4
Kedah Culture, Arts & Tourism Unit
✉ State Secretariat, L2, Blk B, Wisma Darul Aman
☎ (04) 730 1957
⏰ Sat–Wed 8:15–4:45, Thu 8:15–1:15 Museums: Daily 10–6
♿ Free
↔ Langkawi (➤ 20)

 42C1
⏰ All attractions open daily 9–6
🍴 Fast food and hawker stands ($)
♿ None
🎫 Inexpensive; Forest Park: free

 42B2
✉ 13km north of Kuala Lumpur city center
⏰ Daily 7AM–9PM
🍴 Hawker stands ($)
🚌 Bus 11, 70
♿ None
🎫 Temple Cave: free; Art Gallery: inexpensive
↔ Templer Park (➤ 69)

 43D1
🍴 Restaurants in beach resort hotels ($$–$$$)
🚌 Bus from Johor Bahru, ferry from Singapore

 42B3
✉ 104km from KL
☎ (09) 362 2248
🍴 Wide range ($–$$)
🚌 KL to Kuala Kubu Bahru, connecting bus (or taxi)

What to See in Peninsular Malaysia

ALOR SETAR ✪✪
Kedah's state capital retains the charm of its historic core, in spite of moves towards high technology. Here, the graceful, black domes and elegant minarets of the Masjid Zahir, dating from 1912, face the ornate wooden palace of the 19th-century Balai Besar, still used for royal ceremonies. Nearby are the Balai Nobat, where the sacred *nobat* (instruments of Kedah's royal orchestra) are kept, and the Balai Seri Negeri (State Art Gallery). The **Muzium Di Raja** (Royal Museum) houses colorful miniature tableaux of Malay customs and archeological artifacts.

AYER KEROH ✪
Concentrated along the road leading from the North–South Highway to Melaka are several outdoor attractions, including a butterfly farm, a crocodile farm, a boating lake, an aquarium, and the Melaka Zoo. The Mini ASEAN and Mini Malaysia parks have wooden houses built in the styles of the six ASEAN countries (Malaysia, Singapore, Thailand, Indonesia, Brunei and the Philippines) and the 13 states of Malaysia, each with displays of arts and crafts.

BATU CAVES ✪✪✪
Concealed within a towering limestone outcrop, these huge cathedral-like caves were discovered by an American naturalist in 1878. A flight of 272 steps leads to the Temple Cave, whose 100m tall chamber has been used as a Hindu temple for over 100 years. The caves are the focus of the annual Thaipusam festival (➤ 116), when up to 800,000 people celebrate here. A cave at the foot of the outcrop, "the Art Gallery," contains Hindu wall paintings and statues.

CAMERON HIGHLANDS (➤ 25, TOP TEN)

DESARU ✪✪
This 20km beach of golden sand near the southern tip of Peninsular Malaysia is lined with luxury resorts and golf courses, and attracts weekenders from Singapore and Johor Bahru. There is a fishing museum at Tanjung Balau.

FRASER'S HILL (BUKIT FRASER) ✪✪
Named after Louis James Fraser, a 19th-century tin prospector, Fraser's Hill nestles amid the forested highlands at a cool altitude of 1,500m. Fraser ran a gambling and opium den here before it became a hill station in the 1920s. The place still retains a colonial air,

A daunting flight of steps sweeps up the cliff to the hidden Batu Caves

with its neat lawns and rose gardens, nine-hole public golf course and cream teas at the Smokehouse Hotel. Activities include bird-watching, walking, and swimming. There are bungalows, chalets, and two large resorts.

GENTING HIGHLANDS ✪

Genting, from the Chinese for "above the clouds," stands in stark contrast to other Malaysian hill resorts, its twinkling lights clearly visible from KL on a clear night. This is a brash, round-the-clock resort, with a casino, five-star hotels, a cable-car, theme parks, a boating lake, a 16-lane bowling alley, a heated indoor swimming pool, and an international class 18-hole golf course.

🔁 42B2
☎ Reservations and inquiries: (03) 262 3555
🍴 Restaurants in resort hotels ($$–$$$)
🚌 Regular bus service from Puduraya bus station, KL

IPOH ✪✪

The state of Perak (which means 'silver' in Malay) takes its name from the glinting tin ore for which it was once famous. Ipoh, the state capital, was built on the profits of the tin mines, and is today a pleasant city with many colonial legacies. The tree-lined *padang* (square) is overlooked by the mock-Tudor Royal Ipoh Club, and nearby are the elegant façades of the City Hall and the Railway Station. Ipoh nestles among limestone hills, many of which contain cave temples, such as Perak Tong (6km north), and Sam Poh Tong (5km south), with its statues of Buddha.

🔁 42B3
Tourist Information Centre
✉ Jalan Tun Sambanthan
☎ (05) 241 2958
🕐 Mon–Fri 8–4:15, Sat 8–12:45
🔁 Kellie's Castle (▶ 44), Kuala Kangsar (▶ 45)

Mosque in Kota Bharu

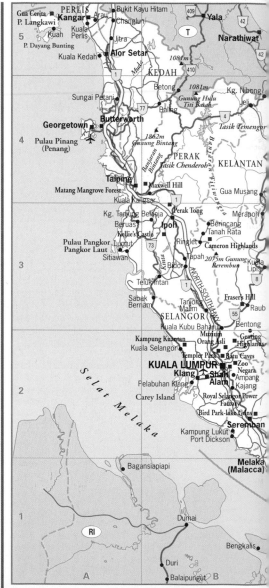

PENINSULAR MALAYSIA

0   50   100   150
Km

Tumpat Pantai Cahaya Bulan
Pasir Pantai Dasar Sabak
Mas Pantai Irama
Sungai Kota Pantai Dalam Rhu
Ko-lok Bharu
Kg. Balang Pasir Puteh P. Perhentian Besar
Merbau Kuala P. Redang
Besut
Kuala Gn. Lawit Merang
Kerai 1519m 3
Dabong Kuala
Terengganu
Lake Kenyir P. Kapas
Tasik Marang
Kenyir Sekayu Waterfalls
TERENGGANU Rantau Abang
Turtle Watching P. Tenggol
Dungun
Taman Negara 3
(National Park) Kerteh
Kuala Tahan
Kg. Kuala Kemaman
Kuala Tembeling Cukai
PAHANG 14 Cherating
Jerantut Panching Kg. Balok
Besera
Kuantan
Maran 3
Temerloh 2 Pahang Pekan
Tasik Cini
Tasik 12
Bera
NEGERI SEMBILAN Nenasi
Bahau
Kuala Pilah Rompin Pulau Tioman
Endau Tekek Juara
Rompin
Segamat Padang
1 3 Pulau
Tampin MELAKA 1036m Rawa
Ayer Keroh Labis Gunung
Tangkak Besar Mersing
Merlimau Muar JOHOR Semberong P. Tinggi
AW 50 Jemaluang P. Sibu Besar
Muar Potteries Keluang
Air Hitam
5 Johor
Batu Pahat 1 Kulai Kota Tinggi
3
Pulau Bengkalis Pontian Johor Bahru Kahang
Kecil SGP Changi
P. Padang C D

Japanese Gardens in Ipoh
(► 41)

🕂 43D1
Muzium DiRaja Abu Bakar
✉ Jalan Air Molek
☎ (07) 223 0555
🕔 Daily 9–6
♿ None
🖐 Expensive
↔ Desaru (➤ 40)

Above: *the gleaming domes of Kuala Kangsar's Ubadiah Mosque*

🕂 43D3
✉ 50km north of Kuantan
🍴 Bars; restaurants near by ($–$$)

🕂 42B3
✉ 12km south of Ipoh, on A8 road between Gopeng and Batu Gajah
🕔 Daily 8.30–7.30
🍴 Café and picnic tables ($)
♿ None
🖐 Inexpensive
↔ Ipoh (➤ 42), Pulau Pangkor (➤ 56)

JOHOR BAHRU ✪

The city of Johor Bahru sits at the southern tip of the peninsula, and serves as a gateway to and from the island-state Singapore via the Causeway. Its hotels and towering malls, including extravagant waterfront developments, cater to weekend shoppers who flock here from Singapore to take advantage of the favorable exchange rates.

The city is worth a visit just to see the **Muzium DiRaja Abu Bakar** (Royal Museum), a 19th-century palace set in beautifully landscaped grounds overlooking the Straits of Johor, a 10-minute walk from the center. Built in 1866 for Sultan Abu Bakar, it is a treasure house of 19th-century Malay and European furniture, china, porcelain, crystal, and *objets d'art*, and evokes the wealth of the Malay sultans.

KAMPUNG CHERATING ✪✪✪

Budget-priced beach-huts, chalets and restaurants line the broad curving bay of Cherating. Though bigger resorts are edging in, it remains a favorite backpackers' beach where bars serve cold beers in the shade of the casuarina trees overlooking the golden sands. The water is shallow and good for swimming at high tide. Asia's first Club Med is around the point to the north, next to Chendor Beach where turtles come ashore to lay their eggs.

KELLIE'S CASTLE ✪✪

This crumbling monument to the unrealized dreams of a wealthy British planter perches on a bluff above a small river. The four-story Moorish mansion was begun in 1915 for William Kellie Smith, but remained unfinished following his death in 1926, and now stands in picturesque decrepitude. Nearby is a small Hindu temple, complete with a figure of Smith on the roof, built to appease evil spirits after several laborers died of a mysterious disease.

KOTA BHARU

The state of Kelantan, in the far northeast of the peninsula, is the cradle of Malay culture. Remote from the commercialized west and south, and with an Islamic state government, Muslim Malay customs and traditions have survived here undiluted. Kota Bharu, the state capital, has interesting historic buildings, colorful markets and craft workshops. Padang Merdeka (Independence Square) lies next to the Kelantan River, surrounded by museums, most notably the wooden palace of the Istana Jahar, built in 1887. More interesting, though, is the Muzium Negeri (State Museum), south of the center. Pasar Besar (Central Market), perhaps Malaysia's most photographed wet market (selling fresh produce and meat), sits on Jalan Temenggung. Head north to get to PCB or Pantai Cahaya Bulan ('Moonlight Beach'). Unfortunately, the beach is not very clean, except for stretches in front of the big resorts, but it is well worth a visit because the road to the beach is lined with Kelantan workshops selling batik, *songket,* colorful kites, woodcarvings, silverware, large fans and wall-hangings.

43C4
Tourist Information Centre
Jalan Sultan Ibrahim
Sun–Thu 8–4:45.
Pantai Desar Sabak (➤ 54), Pantai Dalam Rhu (➤ 54)

Songket *weaving in Kota Bharu*

KOTA TINGGI

The waterfalls at Kota Tinggi are a popular weekend picnic spot for local people, but during the week you can enjoy a swim in the deep, jungle-fringed pool below the upper fall in relative peace. The lower pools are safe for children.

43D1
9km from Lombong, signposted 'Air Terjun'
Daily 8AM–8PM
Restaurant and stands ($)
Inexpensive

KUALA KANGSAR

Kuala Kangsar is a Royal Town (Bandar Diraja), having been the seat of the sultans of Perak since the 18th century. It is famous for its magnificent Ubadiah Mosque, completed in 1917, whose huge, golden onion dome overlooks the river. Nearby is the modern Royal Palace, and the **Muzium Istana Kenangan** (Royal Museum), housed in a wooden palace built in 1926 using neither plans nor nails. This served as temporary accommodation for the sultan while the new palace was built.

42B3
Muzium Istana Kenangan
Jalan Istana, Bukit Chandan
(05) 776 5500
Daily 9:30–5
None
Free
Taiping (➤ 68), Ipoh (➤ 41)

🔢 42B2

✉ 64km northwest of Kuala
  Lumpur

Taman Alam Kuala Selangor

☎ (03) 889 2294

🕐 Daily 9–5 (park 24hrs)

💷 Inexpensive

Kampung Kuantan

✉ 10km east of Kuala
  Selangor

☎ (03) 889 2403
  (reservations, 9–5)

🚤 Boat trips daily 8PM–11PM

💷 Moderate

❓ Package tours from KL
  available

KUALA SELANGOR ●●

This quiet backwater was once the seat of the Bugis
sultans of Selangor, three of whom are buried on the
wooded peak of Bukit Melawati, above the town. The hill
is crowned by a lighthouse and the scant remains of
18th-century Fort Altinberg, overlooking the mouth of the
Selangor River. On the coastal plain below are the
mangrove forests of **Taman Alam Kuala Selangor**
(Kuala Selangor Nature Park), home to hundreds of
species of local and migratory birds. Hides, observation
towers and a boardwalk reward the patient observer with
sightings of monkeys, birds and other animals. Chalet
accommodation is available. **Kampung Kuantan** (10km
upstream) offers boat trips to see the spectacular
evening displays of fireflies.

🔢 43C4

Tourist Information Center

✉ Jalan Sultan Zainai Abidin
  (near Istana Maziah)

☎ (09) 622 1553

🕐 Daily 8.15–4.45

Muzium Negeri

✉ Bukit Losong, 3km south
  of city center

☎ (09) 622 1444

🕐 Daily 9–5. Closed Tue

🍴 Café ($)

🚌 Losong minibus

♿ Few

💷 Moderate

KUALA TERENGGANU ●●

Despite 20 years of oil money, the capital of Terengganu
state has not lost its charming small-town air. Boats still
ferry produce to the lively and colorful jetty fronting Pasar
Besar (Central Market) in the city center.

Down the road in Chinatown, many of the old
shophouses of Jalan Bandar are now used as souvenir
shops, although they have retained their faded dignity.
Resorts and hawker stands remain at a discreet distance
from Pantai Batu Buruk beach.

A big draw is the huge **Muzium Negeri** (State
Museum) complex. Three vast, interconnected halls,
echoing the style of traditional Malay architecture, house
exhibits covering history, nature, decorative arts,
weaponry, ceramics, archeology and Islam. The grounds
contain the Maritime Museum with two traditional
wooden *putera* trading vessels and more humble fishing
boats, as well as four well-preserved wooden houses
with Islamic, Chinese and European design influences.

Above: *the quiet waters
of Kuala Selangor*

KUANTAN ●

The state capital of Pahang is a pleasant city at the
mouth of the Kuantan River. Check out the colorful
waterfront along Jalan Besar, then head 4km out of

🔢 43D3

🍴 Wide range ($–$$)

🚌 39 from Kuantan to Teluk
  Cempedak

---

town to the beach at Teluk Cempedak, a golden strand with several luxury hotels, a lively promenade and plenty of watersports facilities.

MARANG ✪✪

Not to be confused with Merang to the north, Marang is a picturesque fishing village that lies around a narrow lagoon 15km south of Kuala Terengganu.

A popular destination for backpackers for many years, medium-range hotels have now sprung up among the beach-huts and chalets. Though commercialized, its beach is still nice and a good back-to-nature resort sits further south on the 17th Mile. The village of Marang is also the point of departure for Pulau Kapas (➤ 55), clearly visible offshore, and the tiny dive-resort island of Pulau Gemia.

+ 43C4
✉ 125km south of Kuala Terengganu
🍴 Guest-house restaurants overlooking lagoon ($); restaurants at resort hotels ($$)
🚢 Boats to Pulau Kapas can be arranged at hotels
↔ Pulau Kapas (➤ 55)

Maxwell Hill

MAXWELL HILL (BUKIT LARUT) ✪✪

Maxwell Hill is the oldest, smallest and least developed of Malaysia's hill resorts. It is also the wettest place in the country, receiving a drenching 5,000mm of rain each year. The narrow, winding road to the 1,100m summit can be accessed from Taiping by a government-run Land Rover shuttle service only. Limited accommodation is available in a handful of rustic wooden bungalows, and activities rarely go beyond strolling in the gardens and enjoying the views from your veranda.

+ 42B3
Bukit Larut Hill Resort
✉ 12km northeast of Taiping
☎ (05) 807 7241
🍴 Meals available at Maxwell Rest House ($)
🚐 Land Rover shuttle runs hourly, 8–6
♿ None
↔ Taiping (➤ 68)

Melaka

The name Melaka (formerly spelled "Malacca") conjures up romantic images of the Orient: sailing ships at anchor in the strait, cargoes of tea, opium and silk, palm-fringed harbors and the exotic scents of sandalwood and spice. Though long since overtaken by the 20th century, the ancient trading port of Melaka manages to preserve more history than any other Malaysian town.

A worshipper lights a candle at the Cheng Hoon Teng Chinese temple

Founded by a Sumatran prince in the early 15th century, and held at various times by the Portuguese, the Dutch and the British, Melaka has had a long and turbulent history. The old town, Banda Hilir, is clustered around the now silted mouth of the Melaka River, and all the main sights are within easy walking distance. Many of the oldest buildings, such as the Stadthuys, St. Paul's Church, and the fortress gate of A Famosa, are found on and around Bukit St. Paul (St. Paul's Hill). Across the river is Chinatown, a grid of streets lined with shophouses and Peranakan mansions. This is a good area for hunting out antiques and souvenirs and the place to find restaurants and hotels.

Melaka's pot-pourri of cultures is most evident in its cuisine, which betrays influences from Indonesia, China, India, Arabia, and Portugal. The town is best known for Nyonya cuisine, served in a number of restaurants set in old Melaka townhouses. Other delights can be sampled at the hawkers' stands at Gluttons' Corner (► 95).

What to See in the City Center

A FAMOSA ✪✪
When the Portuguese captured Melaka in 1511, they built this fortress to defend their settlement on St. Paul's Hill. The Dutch rebuilt the fortifications in 1670, but in 1808 the British ordered its destruction. Sir Thomas Stamford Raffles, then a government agent in Penang, intervened to preserve the Porta de Santiago gate, which is all that remains today. The stucco relief above the arch commemorates the Dutch renovation (the soldier on the right bears the arms of the Dutch East India Company, "VOC," on his shield).

✚ 43C1
✉ Jalan Kota
↔ Muzium Budaya, St. Paul's Church (▶ 51)

Above: *a detail of the remarkable carving that decorates Cheng Hoon Teng's exterior*

BABA-NYONYA HERITAGE MUSEUM ✪✪✪
This privately owned museum is a monument to the unique Peranakan culture of Melaka. The Babas and Nyonyas (as the men and women respectively are called) are descended from Chinese immigrants who intermarried with local Malays and adopted many of their traditions. This Peranakan mansion was built in 1896 and contains furnishings and artifacts from that period.

✚ 43C1
✉ 50 Jalan Tun Tan Cheng Lock
☎ (06) 283 1273
⏱ Daily 10–12:30, 2–4:30 Guided tour only, duration 45 mins
♿ None
🎟 Moderate

CHENG HOON TENG ✪✪
Malaysia's oldest Chinese temple, dating from 1646 and dedicated to Kuan Yin (goddess of mercy), was built using materials and craftsmen from China. Colorful ceramic sculpture, gilded wood-carving and lacquerwork surround the three altars of Kuan Yin, Ma Cho Po (guardian of fishermen) and Kuan Ti (guardian of tradesmen).

✚ 43C1
✉ Jalan Tokong
⏱ Early till late
↔ Masjid Kampung Kling (▶ 50), Sri Poyyatha Vinayagar Moorthi Temple (▶ 51)

CHRIST CHURCH ✪✪
The bright red façade of Christ Church dominates Town Square in the heart of old Melaka. Built by the Dutch in 1753, it retains its original hand-carved wooden pews, and massive roof beams, each hewn from a single tree-trunk. On the floor are old tombs carved in Dutch and Armenian; more Dutch and British gravestones can be found in the Dutch graveyard at the foot of St. Paul's Hill.

✚ 43C1
✉ Town Square
⏱ Daily
↔ Stadthuys (▶ 51)

MARITIME MUSEUM COMPLEX ★★

Melaka's maritime history is on display in this complex, with its impressive 35-meter-high replica of a 16th-century Portuguese trading ship housing charts and models of ships that used to dock at the port. The adjoining building houses more general maritime exhibits, while across the road, the Royal Malaysian Navy Museum traces naval history and includes recovered relics from wrecks. In the grounds is a former patrol boat.

MASJID KAMPUNG KLING ★★

This mosque, built in 1748, shows an eclectic mix of styles. Sumatran influences are evident in the three-tiered pyramidic roof, but the square, tapered minaret resembles a Moorish tower. The prayer hall contains Corinthian columns and a British Victorian chandelier, and the walls are decorated with English and Portuguese ceramic tiles.

MEMORIAL PERGISTIHARAN KEMERDEKAAN ★
(PROCLAMATION OF INDEPENDENCE MEMORIAL)

Once the premises of the Malacca Club, this 1912 villa is where the British colonialists once gathered. It is now a museum tracing the country's struggle for independence. It fronts the padang (field or plain), where Tunku Abdul Rahman, who became Malaysia's first prime minister, proclaimed the country's independence in 1957. His Chevrolet is on display outside.

MUZIUM BUDAYA (CULTURAL MUSEUM) ★★★

A description in the *Sejarah Melayu* (the 17th-century *Malay Annals*) formed the basis for this magnificent wooden reconstruction of the 15th-century royal palace of the Sultan of Melaka. It was built using traditional carpentry techniques such as dovetail joints. Not a single metal nail was used. This delightful building houses exhibits depicting the sultan's court and other aspects of

Left: *a royal audience re-created in the Muzium Budaya (Cultural Museum)*

Malay culture, including costumes, weapons, musical instruments and traditional games.

ST. PAUL'S CHURCH ⭐⭐⭐

The ruins of this little church enjoy a lovely hilltop setting, shaded by tall trees and looking out over the river to the sea. The church was built in 1521 by the Portuguese who called it Our Lady of the Hill; it was renamed St. Paul's by the Dutch, who abandoned it following the completion of their own Christ Church. St. Francis Xavier preached here in 1545, and his remains were briefly interred here following his death in 1553, before being removed to Goa in India. A marble statue of the saint stands outside.

✛ 43C1
⊠ St. Paul's Hill
↔ A Famosa (➤ 49)

Below: *trishaws parked outside the sturdy Stadthuys*

SRI POYYATHA VINAYAGAR MOORTHI TEMPLE ⭐

Erected in 1781, this was the first Hindu temple built in the country. It is on what is known as 'Harmony Street' – next to it is a Muslim mosque, while up the road is a Buddhist temple. Sri Poyyatha Vinayagar Moorthi Temple was built by the Chitties, Indian traders who married local Malay women.

✛ 43C1
⊠ Jalan Tukang Emas
🕐 Daily
↔ Cheng Hoon Teng (➤ 49), Masjid Kampung Kling (➤ 50)

STADTHUYS ⭐⭐⭐

The Stadthuys, built in the 1650s to house the Dutch governors of Melaka and their offices, is a fine example of 17th-century Dutch colonial architecture, with stout masonry walls, polished wooden floors and louvered windows. Now the Museum of History and Ethnography, displays cover the history of Melaka from its foundation in 1400, and the cultures of Melaka's communities.

✛ 43C1
⊠ Town Square
🕐 Daily 9–6. Closed Fri 12.15–2.45
🍴 Cold drinks vending machine ($)
💲 Inexpensive
↔ Christ Church (➤ 49)

A Walk Around Melaka

Distance
3km

Time
1 hour, excluding time spent visiting attractions

Start point
Tourist Information Office, Jalan Kota
✚ 43C1

End point
Muzium Budaya (➤ 50)
✚ 43C1

Lunch
Heeren House Café ($$)
✉ 1 Jalan Tun Tan Cheng Lock
☎ (06) 281 4241

On this walk you can enjoy striking architecture, historical sites and the hubbub of Melaka's busy center.

Turn left from the tourist office and cross the bridge over the Melaka River into Chinatown. Turn left again at the OCBC Bank along Lorong Hang Jebat, then right at the Heeren House Hotel into Jalan Tun Tan Cheng Lock.

This street is lined with traditional Peranakan mansions, with colorful tiles, carved wooden doors and shutters decorated with golden Chinese characters. Halfway along on the right is the ornate tiled façade of the Baba-Nyonya Heritage Museum (➤ 49).

Continue past Jalan Hang Lekir, and turn right at Jalan Kubu.

Here the main road leads to the tiny Tamil Methodist Church, built in 1908.

Turn right in front of the church into Jalan Tokong, and bear left where the road forks.

The street leads past the Cheng Hoon Teng Temple (➤ 49) on the right.

Turn right along an alley (Jalan Lekiu) in front of the Masjid Kampung Kling to reach Jalan Hang Jebat (formerly Jonkers Street, famed for its antique shops). Go left to reach the bridge and cross back past the tourist office to the Town Square. Go up the covered stairs past the Stadthuys (➤ 51), and up the stairs across the road. Go right along the path at the top to reach St. Paul's Church (➤ 51). Follow the path to the right of the church and descend to A Famosa's gateway (➤ 49) and the Muzium Budaya (➤ 50).

A screen inlaid with mother-of-pearl, displayed at the Baba-Nyonya Heritage Museum

MERLIMAU

The road from Melaka south to Muar passes many fine examples of lovely old Melakan houses, in which Chinese motifs are blended with the traditional Malay style of architecture. These wooden houses are raised on stilts (for ventilation, and to deter snakes and rodents), and have an open veranda at the front with a colorful front staircase, decorated with ceramic tiles. Intricate wood carving embellishes the eaves. Penghulu's House, 2km south of Merlimau, is a fine example of the style. It was built in 1894 for the village chief, and still belongs to his descendants.

43C1
25km south of Melaka
Bus 2 from Melaka to Muar

Above: *a traditional Orang Asli village hut*

MERSING

The bustling fishing port of Mersing is the jumping-off point for exploring the archipelago of coral-fringed islands that lies scattered offshore, including Pulau Tioman and the Johor isles (➤ 65). Mersing's coastal roads offer scenic drives and small resorts make the most of views from cliffs overlooking strings of isles.

43D2
Mersing Tourist Information Office
Jalan Abu Bakar, Mersing
(07) 799 5212
Mon–Fri 9–4, Sat 9–1 Closed Sun

MUZIUM ORANG ASLI

The term *Orang Asli* (literally 'original people') refers to the aboriginal tribes who have inhabited Peninsular Malaysia since prehistoric times. A population of about 60,000 Orang Asli survives today, some maintaining their traditional animist, forest-based lifestyles, others choosing urbanized futures. This small yet excellent museum lies on the road to Genting Highlands, and its collection of old farming tools, blow-pipes, animal traps, weapons, basketry, musical instruments and carved idols provides a fascinating insight into the rapidly-vanishing Orang Asli culture.

42B2
Gombak, 25km north of Kuala Lumpur
(03) 689 2122
Daily 9–5:30
Free

PANTAI DALAM RHU　　　　　　　　😊

Sometimes known as Pantai Bisikan Bayu (Beach of
the Whispering Breeze), this is the prettiest of
Kelantan's beaches, a long stretch of alabaster sand
overhung by the feathery limbs of casuarina trees. It
lies near the fishing village of Semerak (south of Kota
Bharu), and is a 10-minute walk from the road. Closer
to Kota Bharu is Pantai Irama (Melody Beach), near
Bacok. A narrow lagoon separates the sand-spit beach
from a landscaped promenade with a few food and
drinks stands.

PANTAI DASAR SABAK　　　　　　😊😊

On 7 December 1941, more than an hour before the
first bombs fell on Pearl Harbor, the Japanese entered
World War II when they invaded the Malay peninsula by
landing on this peaceful, palm-fringed beach. Today, all
that remains is a crumbling concrete bunker. However,
this is an excellent place to watch droves of colorful
fishing boats, some with their traditional carved *bangau*
prows, motor up the narrow estuary in the mid-
afternoon. There is a flurry of activity when the catch is
quickly unloaded and cleaned before going on sale in
the town markets.

PEKAN　　　　　　　　　　　　😊😊

This pleasantly sleepy town, on the south bank of the
broad Pahang River, is a 'royal town' (Bandar Di Raja),
the seat of the sultans of Pahang. The modern palace
(Istana Abu Bakar) lies about a kilometer back from the
river, surrounded by the immaculate turf of the Royal
Golf Club and the Royal Polo Club, but it is not open to
the public. Head instead for the waterfront, where the

old British Residency houses the **Muzium Sultan Abu Bakar** (State Museum), with displays of royal costumes and jewelry, traditional weapons, Chinese ceramics and natural history. A white-tiled pavilion on a little island opposite the museum contains a display of traditional boat building.

Messing about on the water off the lovely shores of Pulau Kapas

PULAU CAREY ✪
A small settlement of Orang Asli woodcarvers of the Mah-Meri tribe is situated among the oil palm plantations on this island. They have retained their traditional designs, documented by an original reference text written by a German researcher, which carefully detailed the unique lifestyle and crafts of this settlement. The woodcarvers here are famous for their dream spirit masks and the *Moyang Tenong Jerat Harimau* tiger-and-ball sculpture. They also make contemporary works. Their artifacts are on sale in the Cameron Highlands. Access is exclusively by motor vehicle. Nearby is the old Selangor capital of Jugra, which has a lovely 19th-century mosque and palace.

➕ 42B2
✉ 60km west of Kuala Lumpur
🍴 Seafood restaurants by the river ($$)
❓ Visits to the settlement require permits from the Department of Orang Asli Affairs (03) 559 0375

PULAU KAPAS ✪✪✪
A 30-minute boat trip from Marang (➤ 47) takes you to the beautiful little island of Kapas, with its picture-postcard white-sand beaches and sparkling turquoise waters. It is a popular day-trip destination, so if you want peace and quiet, avoid weekends and public holidays. The most popular beaches are on the west coast, but trails lead along the shore and across the island to quieter coves. There is excellent snorkeling around the nearby islet of Pulau Raja. Accommodation is available in several low-key chalet developments.

➕ 43D4
✉ 6km from Marang
🚢 Boat trips can be arranged in Marang
↔ Kuala Terengganu (➤ 46)

PULAU LANGKAWI (➤ 20–1, TOP TEN)

PULAU PANGKOR ✪✪✪

The small island of Pangkor, renowned for its golden beaches, is a popular weekend retreat for city-dwellers; but on weekdays the beaches are less crowded. Pangkor Town, on the east side of the island, is a lively strip of market stands, stores, temples, boatyards and fish-drying racks. A circular road winds to the west coast beaches: Pasir Bogak, in walking distance of the jetty, the backpacker stretch of Teluk Nipah and up north to the pretty Coral Bay. The 17th-century Dutch fort of Kota Belanda is located in the southeast. Pangkor Laut Resort, on a tiny islet, has some of the best beaches – patrons only.

PULAU PERHENTIAN (➤ 23, TOP TEN)

PULAU TIOMAN ✪✪

A good way to get a feel for the forested island is to take a hike across it or a day trip on one of the boats that run tours around its coast. Family-run chalets are plentiful and there is a more up-market three-star resort with a small golf course. There are many good snorkeling areas, but much of the coral close to the resorts has suffered degradation. The small town center of Terek, adjacent to the main jetty and airport, has a small museum and a few stores. A good idea is to take a sea bus to some of the more secluded beaches such as Salang, in the north, Juara, on the east coast, and Nipah and Mukat at the foot of the mountainous south.

Sidebar (Pangkor):

✚ 42A3
✉ Jump off: Lumut, 90km southwest of Ipoh
Tourist Information Centre
☎ (05) 638 4057
♿ None
🚢 20-minute ferry crossing every 15 minutes, 6:30AM–7PM
↔ Kellie's Castle (➤ 44)

Sidebar (Tioman):

✚ 43D2
✉ 60km from Mersing
Tourist Information Centre
✉ Mersing
☎ (07) 799 5212
🕐 Mon–Fri 9–4, Sat 9–1
🍴 Many beach restaurants ($–$$)
🚢 Three ferries a day, usually in the morning (1½ –2 hours)

Pulau Tioman, the largest island along the east coast, offers good snorkeling, diving and trekking

Pulau Pinang (Penang)

Penang, or "Betel Nut Island," is one of Malaysia's favorite tourist destinations. Its varied attractions include the palm-fringed beaches of Batu Feringghi and Teluk Bahang; the panoramic views from Penang Hill; traditional *kampung* (villages); and the lively city of Georgetown, with its historic colonial buildings, many colorful temples and fascinating back streets.

Enjoy the cool breezes and magnificent views from Penang Hill

Penang's strategic location at the northern entrance to the Straits of Melaka has made it an important cargo port since the 18th century, when the British acquired and fortified the island. Now, visitors approaching the island are more likely to be impressed by the rapidly changing skyline against the backdrop of the hills.

The island measures roughly 25km north to south by 15km east to west, and is linked to the mainland by the 13.5km-long Penang Bridge. Georgetown, in the northeast, is an attractive, thriving city of half a million people (▶ 17). The north coast has several good, sandy beaches, though the sea around the island is rather murky compared with the crystal waters of the peninsula's east coast. The coastal plains of the west and south are largely given over to *padi* fields, while the east coast is heavily industrialized along the highway between Georgetown and the international airport at Bayan Lepas. Bukit Bendera (Penang Hill), the highest point on the island, has its own miniature hill resort, complete with a tea kiosk, a hotel, and a funicular railway.

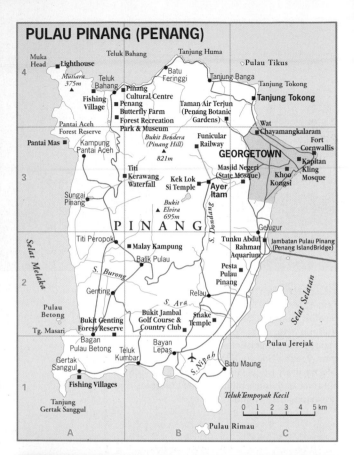

PULAU PINANG (PENANG)

Muka Head
Lighthouse
Teluk Bahang
Tanjung Huma
○Pulau Tikus
4
Mutiara 375m
Teluk Bahang
Batu Feringgi
Tanjung Banga
Tanjung Tokong
Tanjung Tokong
Fishing Village
Pinang Cultural Centre
Penang Butterfly Farm
Forest Recreation Park & Museum
Taman Air Terjun (Penang Botanic Gardens)
Wat
Chayamangkalaram
Pantai Aceh Forest Reserve
Bukit Bendera (Pinang Hill) 821m
Funicular Railway
GEORGETOWN
Fort Cornwallis
Pantai Mas
Kampung Pantai Aceh
Masjid Negeri (State Mosque)
Khoo Kongsi
Kapitan Kling Mosque
3
Titi Kerawang Waterfall
Kek Lok Si Temple
Ayer Itam
Sungai Pinang
Bukit Elvira 695m
P I N A N G
S. Dondang
Gelugur
Selat Melaka
Titi Peropok
Malay Kampung
Tunku Abdul Rahman Aquarium
Jambatan Pulau Pinang (Penang IslandBridge)
Balik Pulau
S. Burong
Pesta Pulau Pinang
2
Genting
S. Ara
Relau
Pulau Betong
Bukit Genting Forest Reserve
Bukit Jambul Golf Course & Country Club
Snake Temple
Tg. Masari
Bagan Pulau Betong
Teluk Kumbar
Bayan Lepas
S. Nipah
Pulau Jerejak
Gertak Sanggul
Batu Maung
Selat Selatan
1
Fishing Villages
Teluk Tempoyak Kecil
Tanjung Gertak Sanggul
0 1 2 3 4 5 km
Pulau Rimau
A
B
C

What to See in Georgetown

CHINATOWN ✪✪✪

Georgetown's Chinatown is the biggest and best preserved in Malaysia. Centered on Lebuh Chulia, its maze of streets is jammed with people, cars, and bicycle rickshaws, and lined with pre-war shophouses, temples, and workshops. You could spend half a day wandering among the back streets, discovering antique stores, rattan-furniture makers, goldsmiths, Chinese coffin workshops, birdcage sellers and clan houses. You'll be assaulted by the everyday sounds and smells of Chinatown – the rattle of moped engines and the clatter of *mahjong* tiles, the sweet fragrance of joss-sticks and jasmine blossom mingling with the aroma of stir-fried meat.

Browsing in Georgetown can yield surprises

➕ 60B1
✉ Lebuh Pantai to Jalan Pinang

FORT CORNWALLIS ✪✪

The crumbling bastions of Fort Cornwallis, which replaced the original timber palisade at the beginning of the 19th century, mark the site of the earliest British settlement on Penang island. Little remains of the fort apart from the ramparts, which are surmounted by a number of ancient cannons. The biggest, known as Seri Rambai, was cast in 1603 and given by the Dutch to the Sultan of Johor. Behind the cannon is the old powder magazine, which houses a small exhibition on the fort's history. The fort sits next to the *padang* (green), overlooked by stately colonial buildings. The ornate clock tower to the south of the fort was presented to the town by a local millionaire to mark the Diamond Jubilee of Queen Victoria in 1897.

➕ 60C2
✉ Lebuh Light
🕐 Daily 8:30–7
🍴 Drinks stall ($)
 ♿ None
🎟 Inexpensive

Opposite page: *intricate Chinese sculpture and art bedeck the magnificent Khoo Kongsi*

KHOO KONGSI ✪✪✪

The most elaborate of Penang's Chinese clan houses was built at the end of the 19th century as a combined meeting hall and temple for the worship of their ancestors. The temple is beautifully decorated with elaborate woodcarvings of Chinese mythical scenes, colorful ceramic tiles and sculptures, and ornate wrought-iron work. The dark-wood interior conceals altars shrouded in incense smoke. A statue of the clan's patron saint sits in the main hall, the God of Prosperity in the left room, and in the right room are gilded ancestral tablets.

➕ 60B1
✉ Cannon Square, off Lebuh Cannon
🕐 Mon–Fri 9–5, Sat 9–1. Closed Sun. (Closed during 2000 for renovations)
 ♿ None
🎟 Free

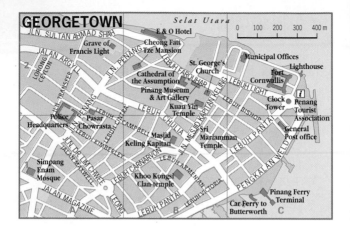

GEORGETOWN

Selat Utara

E & O Hotel
Cheong Fatt Tze Mansion
JLN. SULTAN AHMAD SHAH
Grave of Francis Light
JALAN ARGYLL
LORONG CEYLON
JLN. TRANSFER
St. George's Church
Municipal Offices
Lighthouse
Fort Cornwallis
Cathedral of the Assumption
Pinang Museum & Art Gallery
JLN. PENANG
LEBUH FARQUHAR
LEBUH LIGHT
LEBUH BISHOP
Clock Tower
Penang Tourist Association
Kuan Yin Temple
LEBUH CHULIA
LEBUH CAMPBELL
Police Headquarters
Pasar Chowrasta
LEBUH KIMBERLEY
Masjid Keling Kapitan
Sri Mariamman Temple
LEBUH PANTAI
General Post office
JLN. DR. LIM CHWEE LEONG
JALAN MAXWELL
Simpang Enam Mosque
JALAN MAGAZINE
LEBUH CARNARVON
LEBUH ARMENIAN
Khoo Kongsi Clan-temple
LEBUH VICTORIA
PENGKALAN WELD
LEBUH PANTAI
Pinang Ferry Terminal
Car Ferry to Butterworth

0 100 200 300 400 m

🞙 60B2
✉ Jalan Mesjid Kapitan Keling
🕐 Early morning–late evening
♿ None
🎫 Free
↔ Masjid Kapitan Keling (►below)

🎫 Free, but ask permission from the mosque officials
↔ Kuan Yin Teng (►above)

KUAN YIN TENG (KUAN YIN TEMPLE) ✪✪

Penang's oldest Chinese temple, dating from 1800, is dedicated to the popular goddess of mercy, Kuan Yin, and guarded by two blue ceramic dragons snaking along the ornately decorated roof. Braziers burn in the courtyard, and worshippers bearing joss-sticks and flowers kneel and bow before the altars. The crowd is particularly thick during lunar festivals.

MASJID KAPITAN KELING (KAPITAN KELING MOSQUE) ✪

Rebuilt in 1916, this Moorish mosque, with its distinctive yellow domes, prominent minaret, and symmetrical arches, was founded at the end of the 18th century by

Worshippers praying with joss-sticks at Kuan Yin Teng

the Kapitan Kling, the headman of the South Indian community. The Indian Muslims have traded in the Malay Peninsula since the 11th century. Visitors are welcome, provided they are suitably dressed (➤ 70).

PENANG MUSEUM AND ART GALLERY ✪✪
A statue of Captain Francis Light, the founder of Georgetown, stands in front of the elegant museum building, which dates from 1821. The exhibits chart Penang's colorful history with old photographs, documents, paintings, and engravings, and displays of furniture, costumes, weapons, porcelain, and other items from both the colonial and local communities, including a Chinese bridal chamber and early trishaws. The Art Gallery upstairs showcases local talent and features temporary exhibitions.

ST. GEORGE'S CHURCH ✪
The slender white spire and classical portico of St. George's Church date from 1818. Built using convict labor, it is the oldest Anglican church in Southeast Asia, and sits in a grassy park shaded by the original *angsana* trees that were planted at the time of its construction. The circular pavilion in front of the church is a memorial to Captain Light, who died of malaria in 1794.

WAT CHAYAMANGKALARAM ✪✪
This brightly painted Thai Buddhist temple houses a 33m-long gilded figure of the reclining Buddha, one of the biggest of its kind in existence. The image is guarded by colorful statues of serpents and warriors in the courtyard outside. (Note that no photography is allowed inside the temple.) An equally interesting Burmese temple lies just across the road.

The giant reclining Buddha at Wat Chayamangkalaram

✚ 60B2
✉ Lebuh Farquhar
☎ (04) 261 3144
🕐 Daily 9–5. Closed Fri 12:15–2:45
♿ None
💷 Free
↔ St. George's Church (➤ below)

✚ 60B2
✉ Lebuh Farquhar
🕐 Daily
♿ None
↔ Penang Museum and Art Gallery (➤ above)

✚ 58C3
✉ Lorong Burma, off Jalan Kelawei
🕐 Early morning–late evening
🚌 2, 93, 94, 95
♿ None
💷 Free

61

What to See Around Penang

BATU FERINGGHI   ✪✪✪

Batu Feringghi is Penang's biggest and most famous beach resort. The 3km strand of golden sand is backed by shady casuarina trees and a string of hotels, ranging from luxury to basic, and the main road is lined with restaurants, bars, batik shops, money-changers and car and motorbike rentals. The beach is beautifully clean and well-groomed, but the sea is murky and suffers from pollution; all the hotels have good swimming pools. In the evening the main strip comes alive with market stands and hawkers.

BUKIT BENDERA (PENANG HILL)   ✪✪✪

Penang Hill is one of Malaysia's oldest hill resorts. Its 821m summit was cleared for strawberry-growing soon after the settlement of Georgetown, and quickly became a popular retreat for wealthy colonials, as it is on average 5°C cooler than the coast. Access was by pack-horse or sedan chair until the construction of a Swiss-designed funicular railway in 1923. Today's locally-designed funicular rail journey takes 30 minutes, including a change of trains at the halfway point. The original wooden carriages can be seen at the peak and in the museums at Georgetown and Kuala Lumpur. The summit has a hotel, a mosque, a Hindu temple, and a network of walking trails, including the original road which descends to Jalan Air Terjun near the entrance to the Botanical Gardens (➤ Taman Air Terjun, opposite). The views are especially good around sunset, but the last train down can be very crowded.

BUTTERFLY ✪✪ FARM

This landscaped park with water-falls, rock garden, lily pond, and bubbling mud pool contains thousands of free-flying butterflies, plus displays of other tropical creepy-crawlies such as scorpions, spiders, stick and leaf insects, and giant millipedes.

Sidebar (Batu Feringghi):

- ✚ 58B4
- ✉ 14km northwest of Georgetown
- 🍴 Restaurants and bars ($–$$$)
- 🚌 93
- ♿ Few
- ↔ Teluk Bahang (➤ 63)

Sidebar (Bukit Bendera):

- ✚ 58B3
- ✉ Ayer Itam, 6km west of Georgetown
- ☎ (04) 828 3263
- 🕐 Trains run daily every 30 mins, 6:30AM–9:30PM
- 🍴 Restaurant, tea kiosk ($–$$)
- 🚌 1, 91, 92
- ♿ None
- 👆 Inexpensive
- ↔ Kek Lok Si Temple, Taman Air Terjun (➤ below)

Sidebar (Butterfly Farm):

- ✚ 58A4
- ✉ Teluk Bahang
- ☎ (04) 885 1253
- 🕐 Daily 9–5 (9–6 weekends and hols)
- 🍴 Cold drinks ($)
- 🚌 93
- ♿ None
- 👆 Inexpensive
- ↔ Teluk Bahang (➤ below)

The golden spire of the Pagoda of Ten Thousand Buddhas, in the Kek Lok Si temple complex

KEK LOK SI TEMPLE 😊😊😊

Work on this, the largest of Malaysia's Buddhist temples, began in 1890. It is still being expanded today. The central feature is the 30m-tall Pagoda of Ten Thousand Buddhas with its golden, Burmese-style spire, overlooked by a huge, hilltop statue of Kuan Yin, the goddess of mercy. The complex includes several courtyards, shrines, and pavilions, and a crowded craft and souvenir bazaar.

🚻 58B3
🚌 Ayer Itam, 6km west of Georgetown
🕐 Daily, early till late
🚍 1, 91, 92
♿ None
💰 Free; donation to climb pagoda
🔄 Bukit Bendera (➤ above)

TAMAN AIR TERJUN (BOTANICAL GARDENS) 😊😊😊

Established by the British in 1884, these 30ha gardens incorporate a scenic waterfall and a number of tranquil walks through lush, mature tropical and exotic plant species. Leaf monkeys can be a pest to anyone who appears to be in possession of edible items – picnickers beware! A hiking trail leads to the summit of Penang Hill (➤ opposite).

🚻 58B4
🚌 Jalan Kebun Bunga, 8km northwest of Georgetown
🕐 Daily 7AM–7PM
🍴 Café stalls ($–$$)
🚍 7
♿ Few
💰 Free
🔄 Bukit Bendera (➤ above)

TELUK BAHANG 😊😊

A sleepy village at the end of the north-coast beach strip, with one luxury hotel, souvenir shops, and some natural attractions. Fishing boats land their catches at the long jetty at the west end of the beach, and the village restaurants are famed for their fresh fish and juicy prawns. Hiking trails lead west along the coast as far as the lighthouse on Muka Head, passing some beautiful beaches (which can also be reached by boat from Teluk Bahang – enquire at the fishing village).

🚻 58A4
🚌 20km northwest of Georgetown
🍴 Village restaurants ($–$$)
🚍 93
♿ None
🔄 Butterfly Farm (➤ above)
❓ Cultural shows at Pinang Cultural Centre, daily at 10:15, noon and 8:30

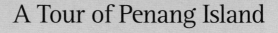

A Tour of Penang Island

Distance
70km

Time
2 hours, not including time
spent at attractions

Start/end point
Georgetown
 58C3

Lunch
Hot Wok Café ($$)
Tanjung Tokong
(04) 899 0858

Inhabitant at the Penang Butterfly Farm

This drive makes an anti-clockwise circuit of the island. Try to get back to Georgetown before the evening rush hour, which begins around 4:30PM.

Leave Georgetown on Jalan Sultan Ahmad Shah.

The route passes the Penang Club and numerous luxurious villas; during colonial times this was called Northam Road, and was home to the city's wealthy merchants.

Follow signs for Tanjung Tokong and Batu Feringghi.

The road winds through the beach-front developments of Tanjung Tokong and Tanjung Bungah, but the best beaches are at the resort of Batu Feringghi (➤ 62).

Another 5km of twisting coastal road leads to Teluk Bahang (➤ 63). At the roundabout in the middle of the village, go straight on to reach the walking trails to Muka Head; otherwise turn left.

The road passes a batik factory, then the Penang Butterfly Farm (➤ 62), before climbing steeply into the fruit- and nutmeg-clad hills. As it begins to descend on the far side, it passes the Air Terjun Titi Kerawang (Titi Kerawang Waterfall), where fruit stalls line the verge. You can stop here and walk a short distance up a path to admire the falls, festooned with luxuriant vegetation.

The road descends to the plain; try the side roads to explore the coastal Malay kampung with traditional stilt houses. Back on the main road follow the signs for Balik Pulau, and then for Bayan Lepas. A turn-off to Batu Maung leads to the shrine built around a footprint said to be that of Cheng Ho, a Chinese explorer . To return to Georgetown, simply follow the highway from Bayan Lepas.

PULAU RAWA AND THE JOHOR ISLES ✪✪✪

Pulau Rawa is one of the numerous tiny islands that dot the seas off Johor. Palm-fringed beaches, clear blue waters, colorful coral reefs, and lush rainforests are the drawcards here. Mersing is the jumping-off point to all the islands except the Sibu isles, which are accessed from Tanjung Leman, 20km south. The biggest island, Pulau Besar, is the closest to the mainland and has lots of chalets. Nearby are Pulau Hujung and Pulau Tengah, with no amenities, but popular with daytrippers. Pulau Rawa has only one resort, but a lovely beach which day visitors can use. Pulau Tinggi is distinguished by a mountain, once important for navigation. There are plenty of chalets here and on Pulau Sibu Besar. Much further on are the tiny fishing islands of Pulau Aur and Pulau Pemenggil.

PULAU REDANG ✪✪✪

A diving paradise, Redang, two hours' boat ride from the mainland, has the most diverse dive sites in the peninsula, with great visibility and good night dive experiences. Marine life includes reef sharks, sea horses, stingrays, and colorful gardens of soft coral. The island is also an important turtle research center, where, contrary to trends elsewhere, populations are actually increasing. Apart from diving, the main attractions are the island beaches of white coral sand, particularly at Pasir Panjang and Teluk Dalam, and the breathtaking sunsets. The island also has a traditional fishing village, a luxury resort and a golf course. Close by is the quieter island of Pulau Lang Tengah, offering snorkeling and leisure diving.

🔲 43D2–D3

🚌 10–05km from Mersing

Mersing Tourist Information Centre

✉ Next to the jetty

☎ (07) 799 5212

🕐 Mon–Fri 9–4, Sat 9–1

🚢 Boats and packages: (07) 799 1222. Scheduled boats only to Pulau Rawa. Arrange at the R&R Plaza (next to jetty) for full board packages or island-hopping day trips.

🔁 Mersing (➤ 53), Pulau Perhentian (➤ 23)

🔲 43C4

✉ 45km from Mersing

🍴 Restaurants in hotels and campgrounds ($–$$$)

🚢 No scheduled boats. Full-board packages only. Inquire at travel agencies at Kuala Terengganu (Jalan Bandar) or dive operators

🔁 Kuala Terengganu (➤ 46), Pulau Perhentian (➤ 23)

Pink anemonefish

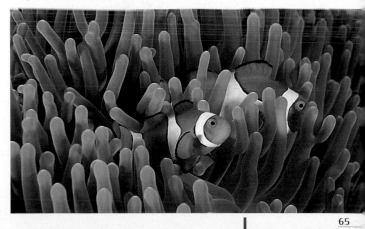

Right and below: *turtles struggle up the east coast beaches of Peninsular Malaysia to lay their eggs*

RANTAU ABANG ✪✪✪
TURTLE SANCTUARY

The east coast of Peninsular Malaysia is one long nesting beach for the four species of sea turtle in Malaysia. The 13-km stretch around Rantau Abang is one of only six known sites in the world where the giant leatherback turtle (*Dermochelys coriacea*) nests. Unfortunately, it is almost extinct, as is the Olive Ridley (*Lepidochelys olivacea*). However, nesting green and hawksbill turtles can be sighted here between May and September. Turtles roam the seas for most of the year (turtles tagged on Malaysian beaches have been found in the Atlantic Ocean), but females return to the same beaches they hatched on, to excavate a hole to lay their eggs, a process that takes several hours. Eight weeks later, tiny hatchlings must make the perilous journey down the beach and out to sea. Only a small percentage of them ever reach maturity. The **Turtle Information Centre** has exhibits and a video on these reptiles and the threats they face. Chalet operators here will wake you up at night if nesting females are spotted. Observe the rules of turtle watching to ensure that the animals are not disturbed while laying their eggs.

✚ 43D4
Turtle Information Centre
⊠ 13th Mile Jalan Dungun
☎ (09) 844 1533
🕐 May–Aug, Sat–Thu 9–11, Sep–Apr, Sat–Wed 8–4,
🚌 Regular buses from Kuala Terengganu and Dungun
↔ Marang (➤ 47)

ROYAL SELANGOR PEWTER FACTORY ✪

The world's largest manufacturer of pewterware was founded in 1885 by a Chinese immigrant to Malaya called Yong Koon, and the family company is still owned by his descendants. The guided tour of the factory allows you to watch craftsmen at work before browsing in the adjoining showroom, outside which stands the world's largest beer tankard – it weighs 1,557kg and can hold 2,790 liters.

✚ 42B2
⊠ 4 Jalan Usahawan Enam, Setapak Jaya, Selangor
☎ (03) 422 1000
🕐 Mon–Sat 8:30–4:45, Sun, public hols 9–4
🚌 167, 169 from KL
✋ Free

SEREMBAN ✪✪

Seremban is the capital of Negeri Sembilan state, which has a unique matrilineal cultural legacy. Immigrants from the Minangkabau region of Sumatra settled in the area, and in the 18th century formed a confederacy to protect themselves from the Bugis sultans of Selangor. The name 'Negeri Sembilan' means 'Nine States' and refers to that ancient confederacy. The Minangkabau people brought with them a distinctive architectural style of upswept, high-gabled roofs, a style echoed in several modern buildings in Seremban and throughout the country. A 19th-century, wooden Minangkabau house can be seen at the **Taman Seni Budaya Negeri** (State Art and Culture Park), along with a wooden Minangkabau palace dating from the 1860s. At the royal capital of Sri Menanti, 33km east of Seremban, is another great architectural feat, the Muzium Diraja Sri Menanti (Royal Museum of Sri Menanti), a museum that sits on 99 pillars.

➕ 42B2
Taman Seni Budaya Negeri
✉ 3km west of city center, at the junction with North–South Highway
🕐 Sat, Sun, Tue, Wed 10–6, Thu 8:15–1, Fri 10–12:15, 2:45–6. Closed Mon
♿ None
🎟 Free

SHAH ALAM ✪

The state capital of Selangor is a planned city of wide roads, landscaped parks and pretty suburbs. It is dominated by the four needle-like minarets and soaring blue dome of the Masjid Sultan Salahuddin Abdul Shah (State Mosque), the largest in the country, capable of accommodating 24,000 worshippers. Nearby is Bukit Cahaya Seri Alam Agricultural Park, with landscaped gardens and walks through showcase plantations and paddy fields.

➕ 42B2
✉ 30km west of KL
🚆 KTM Komuter train to Port Klang

The country's largest mosque, Masjid Sultan Salahuddin Abdul Shah, in Shah Alam

67

The lovely Lake Gardens of Taiping, established in the late 19th century

+ 42A3
Muzium Perak
✉ Jalan Taming Sari
🕐 Daily 9:30–5. Closed Fri 12:15–2:45
♿ None
🎟 Free

TAIPING ✪✪

This predominantly Chinese town was a rowdy, 19th-century tin-mining center, riven by feuds among its Triad secret societies. British authorities clamped down on the unrest in 1874 and called the town Taiping, which means 'Everlasting Peace.' Taiping is best-known for having the country's oldest hill station, Bukit Larut (Maxwell Hill) (► 47), and for its mature, ancient rain tree-lined Lake Gardens (Taman Tasik), incorporating a small zoo and a nine-hole golf course. **Muzium Perak** is the oldest museum in Malaysia, founded in 1883, and has a collection of natural history exhibits, traditional weapons, royal regalia and a good display of Orang Asli artefacts. Taiping also boasts some fine colonial buildings and Perak's oldest Buddhist temple.

+ 42B2
✉ 1km west of Kuala Selangor
☎ (03) 889 2294
🕐 Daily 9–5
🍴 Cold drinks available ($)
♿ None
🎟 Inexpensive

TAMAN ALAM KUALA SELANGOR ✪✪

This 200-hectare nature reserve near the mouth of the Selangor River protects an area of coastal mangrove forest and secondary jungle, centered around a series of man-made lakes. There are several marked nature trails, a couple of observation towers for bird-watchers, and two boardwalks that lead through the mangroves to the coastal mud-flats, where you can see horseshoe crabs and mud-skippers. The secondary jungle, which has grown on drained mangrove swamp, contains troops of macaque and silver leaf monkeys. Otters and monitor lizards are occasionally seen in the lakes. The park's main attraction is its bird life: 156 species have been sighted, including herons, egrets, brahminy kites, woodpeckers, kingfishers, bee-eaters, waders, and waterfowl. Chalet accommodation is available at the park entrance.

TAMAN NEGARA (► 22, TOP TEN)

TASIK CINI (LAKE CHINI)

Set in the wilds of southern Pahang state, this beautiful floodplain of 12 interlocking lakes is said to be inhabited by a giant serpent called Naga Seri Gumum, Malaysia's equivalent of Scotland's Loch Ness Monster. Getting to Cini is an adventure in itself, by road to Kampung Belimbing on the Pahang River, then by boat along the Cini River, beneath a jungle canopy loud with monkeys and brilliant with butterflies and kingfishers. Between June and September, the lakes are carpeted with pretty pink and white lotus flowers. There are also jungle trails and Orang Asli settlements. Lakeside chalets provide basic accommodation.

43C2
100km southwest of Kuantan
Rimba Resort, Tasik Cini
(09) 477 8037
Restaurant at resort ($–$$)
None
Kijang Mas Gumum Resort (Kampung Orang Asli Gumum)
(011) 060700

TEMPLER PARK

Named after its founder, Sir Gerald Templer (Malaya's last British High Commissioner), this 600ha forest reserve is criss-crossed by hiking trails which lead past waterfalls, natural swimming pools, picnic sites, and caves, and is overlooked by the 350m limestone peak of Bukit Takun. Although it's not famed for its wildlife, you can expect to see many species of birds and butterflies, and the common silver leaf monkeys.

42B2
Off Highway 1, 20km north of Kuala Lumpur
Daily, 24 hours
Hawker stands at picnic area near entrance ($)
66 from KL
None
Free
Batu Caves (➤ 40)

ZOO NEGARA (NATIONAL ZOO)

The 65-hectare National Zoo houses a cross-section of Malaysian wildlife in landscaped enclosures with streams and stands of natural forest centered around a lake. Native species on show include tiger, tapir, honey-bear, water buffalo, crocodile, orang-utan and mouse deer. There are also elephants, giraffes, camels and sea-lions, plus an interesting reptile house and aquarium. Entertainment for children includes daily animal shows and elephant, camel and donkey rides.

42B2
Ulu Kelang, 13km northeast of KL
(03) 408 3422
Daily 9–5
Restaurant and hawker stands ($–$$)
170, 177
Moderate

In the Know

If you have only a short time to visit Malaysia, or would like to get a real flavor of the country, here are some ideas:

10
Ways To Be A Local

Learn a few words of Bahasa Malaysia, even if it's only "hello," "please" and "thank you." Any attempt to speak the language will be warmly appreciated.

Start the day with a meal of *roti canai* (fried unleavened bread) washed down with sweet, milky coffee.

Dress respectfully when visiting a mosque: arms and legs must be covered and women must wear a headscarf. Take off your shoes before entering.

Join the crowd at a Hindu or Chinese temple during a festival and learn a little about local religions.

Be aware of points of social etiquette. The following are considered rude: raising your voice, touching someone's head (even a child's), pointing with your finger (Malaysians use a thumb) and kissing in public.

Head indoors or seek out some shade during the heat of midday.

Try your hand at the traditional Malaysian pastimes of top-spinning and kite-flying.

Go to an Open House. Make friends with a Malaysian family and visit them at home during the many festivals.

Have dinner at a hawker center, and sample the delights of cheap and tasty local dishes such as satay and *char kway teow*.

Have your fortune read by a traditional fortune-teller in Kuala Lumpur's Chinatown.

10
Good Places To Have Lunch

Bala's Holiday Chalet ($$) ✉ Lot 55 Tanah Rata, Cameron Highlands ☎ (05) 491 1660. Great home-cooked curries, served in a colonial, stone bungalow.

Bonton ($$–$$$) ✉ 7 Jalan Kia Peng, Kuala Lumpur ☎ (03) 241 3614. Set lunches in Nyonya, Malay and Western styles. Popular with office workers.

Carcosa Seri Negara Hotel ($$$) ✉ Taman Tasik Perdana, Kuala Lumpur ☎ (03) 282 1888. Enjoy a curry tiffin lunch in a splendid colonial villa.

Dulit Coffee House ($$) ✉ Jalan Ban Hock, Kuching ☎ (082) 415588. Oxtail stew, kebabs and other local fare feature at this top eatery.

Green Planet ($–$$) ✉ 63 Jalan Cintra, Georgetown, Pulau Pinang ☎ (04) 261 6192. Stylish and lively coffee-house, popular with travelers, offering good Western and Asian food in pleasant surroundings.

Heeren House ($$) ✉ 1 Jalan Tun Tan Cheng Lok, Melaka ☎ (06) 281 4241. Portuguese and Peranakan food served in an old riverside warehouse.

Nam Heong ($) ✉ Jalan Sultan, Kuala Lumpur. Cantonese-style noodles, beancurd innovations and a variety of stir-fried dishes served with rice.

Nan Xing ($$) ✉ 33 Jalan Haji Samon, Kota Kinabalu ☎ (088) 212900. Dim sum and top-class Chinese seafood dishes served in an air-

conditioned restaurant. Recommended.

Pot Bless Restaurant ($$) ✉ Hutton Lane, Penang ☎ (04) 263 7984. Help-yourself steamboat soup meal with vegetables and meats at this popular restaurant.

Pulau Tikus Hawker Centre ($) ✉ Pulau Tikus (near the market), Penang. Tasty hawker delights, including *chee cheong fun* noodles, *loh bak* meat salad and curries.

10
Top Activities

Bird-watching: Malaysian Nature Society ✉ 641 JKR, Jalan Kelantan, 50480 Kuala Lumpur ☎ (03) 287 9422

Golf: Malaysia is a top golf venue (► 114)

Jungle-trekking: Try Adventure ✉ 31M, Jalan Bukit Idaman 8/1, 68100 Batu Caves, Selangor ☎ (03) 6137 9221 (► 115)

Kite-flying: Kelantan State Tourist Information Centre ✉ Jalan Sultan Ibrahim, 15050 Kota Bharu, Kelantan ☎ (09) 748 5534

Leisure driving: Hire a car and take advantage of Malaysia's excellent road system to explore out-of-the-way towns and villages as well as some of the best of nature.

Picnicking: Besides a variety of national parks and beaches, there is a plethora of forest recreation parks with good public amenities.

River safari: Sarawak Tourist Information Centre

Above: *Taman Negara transport*
Opposite: *traditional wood-carving in progress*

✉ 31 Jalan Masjid, Kuching ☎ (082) 410944 (► 88)

Scuba-diving and snorkeling: Malaysia's coral islands are protected as marine parks and many operators run diving and snorkeling trips. (► 115)

Theater: Actors' Studio ✉ Plaza Putra (beneath Dataran Merdeka), Kuala Lumpur ☎ (03) 294 5400

Turtle-watching: The top spots are Turtle Islands (► 79), Rantau Abang (► 66), and Pulau Redang (► 65).

10
Best Beaches

- Bako National Park
- Juara, Pulau Tioman
- Marang
- Pantai Kok, Langkawi
- Pantai Tanjung Rhu, Langkawi
- Pasir Panjang, Pulau Perhentian Kecil
- Pulau Pangkor
- Pulau Redang
- Tuanku Abdul Rahman National Park, Sabah
- Turtle Islands National Park, Sabah

5
Top Viewpoints

- Bukit Bendera (Penang Hill), Penang
- Civic Centre, Kuching, Sarawak
- Gunung Brinchang, Cameron Highlands
- Menara KL, Kuala Lumpur
- Mount Kinabalu summit, Sabah

5
Famous Hawker Centers

- Gluttons' Corner, Jalan Taman Merdeka, Melaka
- Gurney Drive, Georgetown, Penang
- Jalan Alor, Bukit Bintang, Kuala Lumpur
- Pasar Malam, Jalan Padang Garong, Kota Bharu
- Wooley Centre, Ipoh Garden, Ipoh

East Malaysia

The states of Sarawak and Sabah, known together as East Malaysia, cover an area of northern Borneo almost twice the size of Peninsular Malaysia. Separated from the mainland by the South China Sea, this is a vast, wild, and adventurous country, where you can climb the highest mountain between New Guinea and the Himalayas, explore the world's largest cave chamber, see the world's largest flower and visit one of the oldest known human habitations in Southeast Asia. The chief cities of Kuching and Kota Kinabalu serve a hinterland of mountain and forest, home to a range of indigenous peoples, from the former head hunters of the Iban, to the Kadazandusun and Bajau Laut, the 'sea gypsies' of the Malay Archipelago. Expeditions up the Skrang and Rajang rivers to the longhouses of the Iban of Sarawak are popular excursions from Kuching. Sabah's coral islands are among the world's top dive destinations.

> *'Hundreds of butterflies...floating, flapping ...in small bursts, gliding, fluttering like bats...made their way towards us and settled on our boots and trousers...'*

REDMOND O'HANLON
Into the Heart of Borneo (1984)

29E/F2
Sabah Tourism Promotion Corporation
 51 Jalan Gaya, Kota Kinabalu; PO Box 10626
☎ (088) 212121
🕐 Mon–Fri 8–5, Sat 8–2. Closed Sun

Muzium Sabah
✉ Jalan Muzium, 3km south of city center
☎ (088) 253199
🕐 Daily 9–5
🍴 Cafeteria ($)
♿ Few
 Free

Gaya Street Sunday Market
✉ Jalan Gaya
🕐 Sun 7–11

Filipino Market
✉ Jalan Tun Fuad Stephens
🕐 Daily 8–9

House of Skulls
✉ Kampung Monsopiad, Penampang
☎ (088) 761336
🕐 Daily 9.30–5

Opposite: *a medicine man prepares to advise his patients in a Sabah market*

Sabah

Sabah is known as the "Land Below the Wind," lying as it does just south of the typhoon belt. It is a land of rugged mountains, fringed by coastal swamps and coral islands, bordered to the south by Sarawak and the Indonesian state of Kalimantan. Kota Kinabalu, the capital of Sabah, can be reached by air from Kuala Lumpur and Johor Bahru.

Rich stocks of tropical hardwood attracted the British North Borneo Company, who administered the territory from 1881 until World War II. After the war, North Borneo became a British Crown Colony, and finally joined Malaysia as the state of Sabah in 1963.

Sabah appeals to outdoors enthusiasts, offering superb scuba diving, jungle trekking, mountain climbing and white-water rafting. Its national parks protect rare and exotic plant and animal life such as orang-utans, proboscis monkeys, hornbills and the *Rafflesia*, the world's largest flower.

Kota Kinabalu, the state capital, was flattened by bombing during World War II, and the new city developed around a grid of soulless concrete blocks. KK, as it is commonly known, is best used as an entry point – it has an international airport – and is the jumping-off point to the state's many attractions, which are most quickly accessed by air. The other main cities are Sandakan and Tawau. Travel arrangements can be made through the many tour agencies and permits and accommodation can be obtained through Sabah Parks agents.

A good introduction to Sabah is gained from a visit to the **Muzium Sabah**, in the south of KK. Its Ethnic Gallery showcases the cultures of indigenous tribes, the largest of which are the Kadazadusun, Murut, and Bajau. Archive photos, documents and newspapers tell the story of Sabah's colonial and wartime history. Less intellectual pursuits are catered for at the golden strand of Tanjung Aru beach, also to the south. On the same road as Sabah Tourism is the **Gaya Street Sunday Market**, while the **Filipino Market** sits on the waterfront next to the Central Market. Down this stretch are the jetties for the Tunku Abdul Rahman Park (➤ 79) and Labuan. Penampang, 13km from the city center, is Kadazandusun heartland. At the end of May, the colorful harvest festival is celebrated here, with traditional ceremonies and Christian prayers. The **House of Skulls** at nearby Monsopiad relates local head-hunting history.

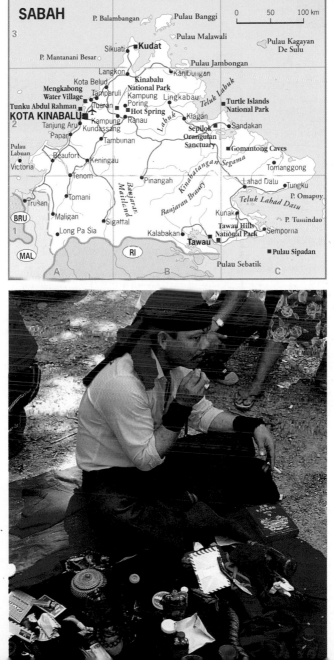

What to See in Sabah

GOMANTONG CAVES ✪✪

These limestone caves, about 32km inland on the far side of the bay from Sandakan, have for centuries been harvested for their swiftlets' nests, the raw ingredient of the famous Chinese delicacy, birds'-nest soup. The tiny nests are collected from the cavern roofs by agile collectors who climb up precariously rigged bamboo poles and rattan ropes to reach their goal. (The harvesting seasons are February to April and July to September.) There are two caves: Simud Hitam, a five-minute walk from the Information Centre, and Simud Putih, an hour's hike up the mountain. This cave provides the even more valuable white nests, made of pure saliva, that are worth around US$500 a kilogram. Visitors must obtain a permit from the **Wildlife Department** office in Sandakan.

KINABALU NATIONAL PARK (► 18, TOP TEN)

KUDAT ✪

Located on the northern tip of Sabah, this area is the homeland of the Rungus people, famed for their handicrafts. Some longhouses here are open to visitors. By day, womenfolk spin and embroider material, thread elaborate beadwork, and weave baskets. Cultural shows are performed in the evening.

PADAS GORGE ✪✪

The gorge of the Padas River cuts through the southern end of the Crocker Range between the towns of Tenom and Beaufort, and offers an exhilarating expedition for white-water rafters. Packages usually include a charming two-and-a-half-hour ride on East Malaysia's only railway line from Tenom to Beaufort (► 111).

PORING HOT SPRINGS ✪✪✪

Set in the eastern foothills of Mount Kinabalu, the sulphurous hot springs at Poring are popular with climbers who have just returned from an ascent of the mountain. Having soothed your aching muscles in the outdoor hot tubs, built by the Japanese during their World War II occupation, you can cool off in the swimming pool, before exploring the surrounding forest. As well as the ordinary hiking trails, there is an exciting rope-walk, suspended 30m up in the rainforest canopy. Hostel and chalet accommodation must be booked through Kinabalu Gold Resorts in Kota Kinabalu (► 18).

Sidebar (Gomantong Caves):

✚ 75C2
Wildlife Department
✉ 6th floor, Urusetia Building, Batu 7, Labuk Road, Sandakan
☎ (089) 666550
🕐 Daily 8–4
🍴 Picnic site beneath caves; cafeteria ($)
❓ Boat from Sandakan (2 hours), then Land Rover (best by organized tour)
♿ None
🎫 Permit from Wildlife Department, inexpensive

Sidebar (Kudat):

✚ 75B3
🚌 Regular buses from Kota Kinabalu (4 hours)

Sidebar (Poring Hot Springs):

✚ 75B2
✉ 19km north of Ranau
🕐 Baths: daily 7AM–6PM; rope-walk: daily 10–4
🍴 Cooking facilities only
🚌 Minibus from Ranau or Kinabalu Park HQ
♿ None
🎫 Baths: inexpensive; free for overnight guests
↔ Kinabalu National Park (► 18)

SANDAKAN AND THE KINABATANGAN BASIN ✪✪

Sandakan was founded in 1879 as a timber town and in 1884 it became the capital of the newly established territory of British North Borneo. The town was occupied by the Japanese during World War II, and completely razed by Allied bombing at the end of the war, after which the capital was transferred to Kota Kinabalu. The region around Sandakan has been famous for centuries as a source of exotic natural treasures such as edible birds' nests, pearls, camphor and sea cucumbers. Today it is a gateway to the wildlife attractions of Gomantong Caves (➤ 76), Sepilok Orang Utan Sanctuary (➤ 78), and Turtle Islands National Park (➤ 79). Two hours' drive from Sandakan is Sakau, the base for exploring the lush Kinabatangan basin, perhaps the best place in Malaysia to observe animals in the wild. The area's star attraction is the unusual proboscis monkey, which can be observed from boats in the evenings. Tours up the many rivers pass through diverse Bornean rainforests which offer excellent birdwatching opportunities.

🚑 75C2
Sabah Parks Office
✉ 9th floor, Wisma Khoo Siak Chew, Jalan Buli Sim Sim, Sandakan
☎ (089) 273453
🕐 Mon–Thu 8–12.45, 2–4:15; Fri 8–11:30, 2–4:15; Sat 8–12.45. Closed Sun

Relaxing in the therapeutic waters of Poring Hot Springs

75C1
Borneo Divers
✉ 4th floor, Wisma Sabah, Kota Kinabalu
☎ (088) 222226

SEMPORNA AND PULAU SIPADAN ✪✪

This town at the far southeastern frontier of Sabah is built half on land, half on stilts and jetties extending out over the sea. It has a lively seafood market frequented by the local Bajau Laut 'sea gypsies' but the main reason for visiting is to catch a boat to the marine reserve of Pulau Sipadan, 40km offshore. Sipadan is a world-famous scuba-diving site, a submerged limestone peak capped by a fringing coral reef. On the east side of the island, 'The Wall' drops almost vertically from the surface to a depth of 600m. The waters around Sipadan abound with spectacular marine life that includes barracuda, turtles, moray eels, white-tip sharks, whale sharks and a myriad multi-colored tropical fish. Trips to the reserve are best organized through dive operators such as **Borneo Divers** in Kota Kinabalu.

Life on the ocean waves: the houses of Semporna are built over the sea

 75B2
✉ 25km west of Sandakan
🕐 Sat–Fri 9–12 (Fri 11:30), 2–4; feeding times 10AM and 3PM
🍴 Cafeteria ($$)
🚌 Sepilok bus from Sandakan, or taxi
♿ None
✋ Moderate

SEPILOK ORANG-UTAN SANCTUARY ✪✪✪

Sabah's best-known wildlife attraction was set up in 1964 to rehabilitate captive and orphaned orang-utans to the wild. These red-haired apes are one of humankind's closest living relatives, and are under threat from poachers, logging operations and the destruction of their rainforest habitat for agriculture.

The Visitor Information Centre near the park entrance shows videos explaining the main objectives of the sanctuary, but the top attraction tends to be the feeding platforms. Younger primates are given their twice-daily refreshments not far from the Information Centre. Older ones call in for their meal of milk and bananas at a platform deeper in the forest, a 30-minute hike away. There are a couple of hiking trails through the forest reserve around the sanctuary.

 75B1
🍴 Wide range of hawker stands and restaurants ($)
🚌 One bus daily from Sandakan (six flights daily from Kota Kinabalu)

TAWAU ✪

Tawau is a small but booming commercial port in the wilds of southeastern Sabah, making a living from the export of palm oil, cocoa and timber. An hour's drive to the north is the Tawau Hills National Park, a region of rugged volcanic hills, criss-crossed with jungle trails.

Just hanging around: an orang-utan tests its biceps at the Sepilok sanctuary

TUNKU ABDUL RAHMAN NATIONAL PARK ✪✪✪

The five coral islands of this national park lie only a few kilometers offshore from Kota Kinabalu. They are covered in dense jungle and have beautiful beaches of white coral sand, while the fringing reefs offer excellent snorkeling and scuba-diving. The nearest island, Pulau Gaya, is only 15 minutes by boat from Kota Kinabalu, and all are within reach by day trip. Chalet accommodation is available on Pulau Manukan and Pulau Mamutik, and camping is allowed on the other islands provided you obtain an official permit. All overnight stays must be arranged through the Sabah Parks Office in Kota Kinabalu (➤ 77).

🚩 75A2
🍴 Restaurant on Pulau Manukan ($)
🛥 Ferry service from jetty next to central market
🚻 None
🎟 Park admission, inexpensive

TURTLE ISLANDS NATIONAL PARK ✪✪✪

A group of tiny coral islands about 40km north of Sandakan is one of the most important nesting grounds for turtles in Southeast Asia. Three of the islands – Pulau Selingan, Pulau Gulisaan and Pulau Bakungan Kecil – were designated as a national park in 1977 to protect the hawksbill and green turtles that crawl ashore to lay their eggs in the white coral sand. Turtles visit the islands all year round, but the peak nesting season for hawksbills is February to April; for green turtles, July to October. Limited accommodation is available on Pulau Selingan, and all visits must be organized through tour operators or Crystal Quest in Sandakan. Day trips are not possible.

🚩 75C2
Crystal Quest
✉ Rm 1204, 12th Floor, Wisma Khoo Siak Chew, Jalan Buli Sim Sim, Sandakan
☎ (089) 212111
🍴 Restaurant on Pulau Selingan ($)
🛥 Organized boat trips only
🚻 None

Food & Drink

One of the main attractions of a holiday in Malaysia is the opportunity to sample the wide range of delicious and exotic dishes sold in roadside stands, coffeeshops and hotel restaurants. Malaysian cuisine has been influenced by contact with the cultures of Thailand, China, Indonesia, India, the Middle East, and Portugal, yet is still based firmly on local produce.

Malay

The national dish, available at almost every hawker center, is satay – tiny kebabs of chicken, beef or goat marinated in spices, barbecued over glowing coals, and served with a spicy peanut sauce. Rice (*nasi*) can be steamed or cooked in coconut milk (*nasi lemak*) or fried (*nasi goreng*). The popular breakfast of *nasi lemak* is rice cooked in coconut milk, accompanied by egg, peanuts, cucumber and crunchy, deep-fried anchovies (*ikan bilis*). Fish is very popular, and is usually grilled whole (*ikan bakar*), while beef and chicken are often served in spicy, coconut curry sauce such as *rendang* or *percik*. A classic dish from northern Peninsular Malaysia is *laksa*, a rich, spicy soup made with prawns, *belacan* and bean-sprouts with rice noodles; a Peranakan variation from Melaka (*laksa lemak*) is flavored with coconut cream. A meal at a hawker center can be washed down with soy-bean drink, sugar-cane syrup, or freshly prepared tropical fruit juice – guava, lime, pineapple, papaya, mango, starfruit – or the unusual Malaysian dessert called *ais kacang*, which is a sweet cocktail of shaved ice, syrup, condensed milk, jelly cubes and beans.

Mouth-watering snacks on offer at a Kuala Lumpur street stand

Indian

The Indian community in Malaysia originated largely in the south of the country, where the Hindu Tamil food is mainly vegetarian. Vegetable curries are served on banana-leaf

"plates," accompanied by a mound of steamed rice, and eaten using the fingers of the right hand. Northern Indian cuisine is based on chicken and mutton, marinated in yoghurt and spices, and cooked in a clay oven called a tandoor. Such tandoori meals are accompanied by breads such as naan, *paratha* and chapati cooked in the tandoor.

Delicious and cheap Indian snacks include *murtabak*, a 'pancake' of paper-thin bread dough stuffed with egg and a choice of meat or vegetables; *samosa*, a pastry parcel of spicy meat and/or vegetables; and *roti canai*, a popular breakfast dish of lightly fried *murtabak* dough with a bowl of *dahl* (spiced lentils) or curry gravy as a dip.

Above: a pick-and-mix tray of Nonya kuih (cakes) in Georgetown

Chinese

Chinese food comes in many regional variations, from the Cantonese and Beijing cuisines familiar in the west to the less well-known specialties of Hainan, Sichuan, Hokkien and Teochew. Classic Chinese hawker dishes include Hainanese chicken-rice, which is as simple as it is delicious: steamed or fried chicken served with a clear chicken soup: steamed rice and vegetables, with ginger and chilli sauce on the side; and *char kway teow*: fried flat noodles with prawns or meat, vegetables and a spicy sauce. *Dim-sum*, stuffed dumplings and soupy noodles are typical breakfast fare.

Below: hearty noodle dishes are popular throughout the day

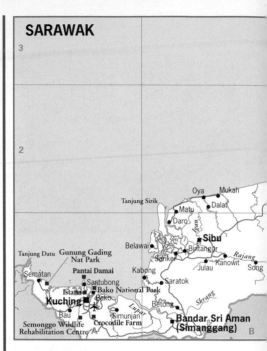

SARAWAK

Oya • Mukah
Tanjung Sirik • Matu • Dalat
• Daro
Sibu
Belawai • Binatangor
Tanjung Datu Gunung Gading   Sarikei   *Rajang*
Nat Park
Semátan   **Pantai Damai**   Kabong   • Saratok   Julau   Kanowit   Song
• Santubong
Istana • **Bako National Park**
Kuching • Bako   • Betong   *Skrang*
Bau   • Simunjan   *Lupar*
Semonggo Wildlife   Crocodile Farm   **Bandar Sri Aman**
Rehabilitation Centre   **(Simanggang)**

**Visitors Information Centre
Kuching**

 31 Jalan Masjid, Kuching

 (082) 410944

 Mon–Thu 8–4:30, Fri
8–4:15, Sat 8–1. Closed
Sun

? Also houses the National
Parks and Wildlife Office

**Sarawak Tourist
Association**

✉ Main Bazaar, Kuching

☎ (082) 240620

Sarawak

**Sarawak is Malaysia's largest state, occupying an
area of northwestern Borneo that is almost the size
of England, but with a population of only 1.5
million. It is bordered to the south and east by the
Indonesian state of Kalimantan, and to the north
by Sabah and the tiny, oil-rich kingdom of Brunei.**

Sarawak was once a province of the sultanate of Brunei,
but in 1841 the English adventurer James Brooke declared
himself Rajah of Sarawak, after helping to suppress a
revolt. Brooke and his descendants ruled Sarawak as the
famous "White Rajahs" until World War II, after which the
territory was ceded to the British crown, before finally
joining the Federation of Malaysia in 1963.

Kuching, the state capital of Sarawak, is one of
Malaysia's most interesting and enjoyable cities, with an
attractive waterfront, colorful streets and the country's
best museum (➤ 19). The Malay word *kucing* means
"cat," a fact celebrated by a number of cat sculptures
scattered across the city, but the name probably derives
either from the Chinese word *kochin*, meaning "harbor,"
or from the *mata kucing* tree (the "cat's eye" fruit) which
is widespread along the river banks. Although there are

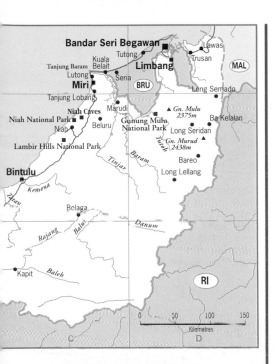

good roads in the cities, the boat remains the most important mode of transport in Sarawak, both along the coast and inland up the many navigable rivers. However, the quickest way to cover the huge distances is on one of the many scheduled air services. The main attractions are the spectacular national parks of Bako, Gunung Mulu, and the Niah Caves, and the tours upriver to visit the traditional native longhouses.

Boats on the Sarawak River, near Kuching

What to See in Kuching

CHINESE HISTORY MUSEUM ✪

This little museum, on the waterfront opposite the Tua Pek Tong temple, charts the history of Sarawak's large Chinese community from the days of the earliest traders through the Brooke period and into modern times.

82A1
✉ Main Bazaar
🕐 Sat–Thu 9–6. Closed Fri
Free

FORT MARGHERITA ✪✪

A *tambang* (ferry) will take you across the river, from the steps below the Square Tower, to visit this relic of the White Rajahs. The fort was built in 1879 to guard the river against pirates, and was named after Margaret, the wife of the second rajah, Charles Brooke. Now a Police Museum, it has weapons and uniforms, relics of the

82A1
🕐 Tue–Sun 10–6. Closed Mon and public hols
🚢 Ferry from steps below Square Tower
♿ None
Free

Above: the striking white stone of Fort Margherita gleams above the trees

Japanese occupation and a re-created opium den. Upstream from the fort, on the same bank, is the Astana, an elegant palace built for Charles Brooke in 1870 and now the official residence of Sarawak's head of state.

KAMPUNG BUDAYA SARAWAK (SARAWAK CULTURAL VILLAGE) ✪✪✪

Dramatically set against the Santubong mountains, this sprawling "living museum" of excellent native architecture shows Sarawak at a glance, complete with demonstrations of traditional lifestyles, from weaving to music, blowpipe-making to sago-processing. Built to preserve

82A1
✉ Damai, 30km north of Kuching
🕐 Daily 9–5:15, Cultural Show 11:30, 4:30
🍴 Restaurant ($)
🚌 From Jln Gambier; tours

and promote ethnic heritage, it may appear commercial, but it provides an excellent opportunity to experience a culture that is difficult to access and, in many cases, is dying out. There are native guides in full regalia in each tribal house. The entrance fee covers a cultural performance staged by the village's dance troupe.

MAIN BAZAAR ✪✪

Charming antique and handicraft shops line Kuching's oldest street, opposite the waterfront. This is where you can select from a huge range of primitive art, reproductions, and contemporary souvenirs and knick-knacks. The parallel road of Jalan Carpenter, with its little shops and lanes, is also interesting to wander through.

- 🔲 82A1
- ✉ Main Bazaar
- 🕐 Daily 9–6
- 🍴 Coffeeshops ($)
- ✋ Free

SARAWAK MUSEUM ✪✪✪

Kuching is fortunate to have probably the richest and most varied museum collection in Malaysia, if not in the whole of Southeast Asia. The collection is displayed in two buildings. The Old Building, opened in 1891, houses an extensive natural history exhibition, which includes many items collected during the 19th century under the direction of British naturalist Alfred Russel Wallace. It also has a magnificent ethnographic collection, which includes a reconstruction of an Iban longhouse complete with shrunken heads. A footbridge leads over the road to the New Building, which has more ethnographic exhibits, a display of Chinese ceramics, and a re-creation of one of the Niah Caves. There is also a good bookshop and souvenir store. The grounds behind the Old Building contain botanical gardens and an aquarium.

- 🔲 82A1
- ✉ Jalan Tun Abang Haji Openg
- ☎ (082) 258388
- 🕐 Mon–Thu 9:15–5:30, Sat–Sun 9:15–6
- ♿ None
- ✋ Free

TIMBER MUSEUM ✪

This wooden building contains a range of exhibits on Sarawak's various forest types, the commercial timber industry, and natural produce of the rainforests. The history and development of the state's century-old timber industry are outlined, as are the current management practices which attempt to assure that all is well. There is also a research library.

- 🔲 82A1
- ✉ Wisma Sumber Alam, Petra Jaya
- 🕐 Mon–Thu 8:30–4, Fri 8:30–11:30, Sat 8:30–12:30. Closed Sun

TUA PEK KONG ✪

Kuching's oldest Chinese temple dates from the 1840s, and is probably the city's oldest surviving building. It is brightly decorated, with red walls and green steps guarded by blue and gold ceramic dragons, and there is always a handful of devotees lighting joss-sticks or burning paper money and making invocations to the God of Prosperity.

- 🔲 82A1
- ✉ Corner of Jalan Tunku Abdul Rahman and Jalan Padungan
- 🕐 Early morning–late evening

A Walk Around Kuching

Distance
3km

Time
1 hour, not including time
spent visiting attractions

Start point
Visitors' Information Centre,
Padang Merdeka
✚ 82A1

End point
Sarawak Museum
✚ 82A1

Lunch
Chinese Food Centre ($)
✉ Jalan Carpenter (opposite
the temple)

Mosques, temples and historical buildings feature in this walk, which also takes in the city's waterfront.

From the Visitors' Information Centre, walk left along Jalan Masjid and head toward the golden domes of the Masjid Kuching (Kuching Mosque). Turn right at the mosque, left into Jalan Power and right into Jalan Gambier.

The route passes the fish and vegetable markets. The start of the waterfront is marked by the Square Tower, a tiny fort built in 1879. On the right is the 19th-century Court House complex, the seat of Sarawak's first government, which comprises the stately court house, clock tower, pavilion, Round Tower, and a memorial to Rajah Charles Brooke.

Stroll along the waterfront, a landscaped esplanade that is a great place to observe local people at leisure.

There are views across the river of the Astana and Fort Margherita (➤ 84); pop into the Chinese History Museum. The Esplanade ends at the Riverside Majestic Hotel.

Kuching's market is full
of wonderfully fresh
produce

Back-track, then cross the main road to get to the colorful Tua Pek Tong temple. Follow the main road, turn left into Jalan Wayang, then right again at another Chinese temple into Jalan Ewe Hai, which becomes Jalan Carpenter, lined with 19th-century Chinese shophouses. At the junction, turn left into Jalan Tun Abang Haji Openg.

This road leads to the Sarawak Museum, past the magnificent neo-classical General Post Office.

The museum is after the Padang; the old wing is on the left.

What to See in Sarawak

BAKO NATIONAL PARK ✪✪✪
The park's remarkable sandstone sea cliffs, huge variety of plants and animals, and secluded beaches are easily accessible from Kuching, by boat from Bako. Among the attractions are monkeys, including the rare proboscis monkey, bearded pigs, and numerous bird species. There are different grades of trails. Besides chalets, dorms and campsites, there is a canteen and information center. Permits and bookings must be made at the Visitors' Information Centre in Kuching.

BARIO ✪✪✪
Bario is the gateway to the ruggedly beautiful and remote Kelabit mountains, home to Sarawak's hill tribes. The Kelabit are the only tribes to practice wet paddy cultivation and Bario rice is considered the best rice in Sarawak. Trekking is the main attraction, with overnight stays at the large Kelabit longhouses. Experienced climbers would enjoy Gunung Murud (2,424m) and Batu Lawi (2,043m).

GUNUNG GADING NATIONAL PARK ✪✪
This nature reserve, a two-hour drive west of Kuching, is home to many species of rare plants, including the spectacular earth star, or *Rafflesia*, the world's largest flower. It was named after Sir Thomas Stamford Raffles, the founder of Singapore, who was the first to record a

---

✚ 82A1
✉ 37km from Kuching, then 20 minutes by boat
🍴 Canteen ($)
🚌 Regular buses from Lebuh Market, Kuching
✋ Permits compulsory, inexpensive

✚ 03D2
Visitors' Information Centre
✉ 452 Jalan Melayu, Miri
☎ (085) 434181
🕐 Mon–Thu 8–4:30, Fri 8–4:45, Sat 8–1. Closed Sun
✈ Regular flights to Miri and Marudi
🔁 Miri (➤ 89), Gunung Malu National Park (➤ 88)

The coastline at Bako National Park is spectacular

82A1

Near Lundu, about 70km west of Kuching

Park HQ: (082) 735714

Regular buses from Lebuh Jawa, Kuching

Park fees, cheap

83D2

Mulu National Parks HQ

(085) 434561

National Parks and Wildlife Office

Jalan Puchong, Miri

(082) 463367

Right: *children peering down from their longhouse*

Far right: *morning wash down at the river*

description of this remarkable plant. The *Rafflesia* is a parasite, growing on the roots of forest vines, and the plant's body is invisible, a mere network of thin strands penetrating the body of its host. The flower, however, is up to one meter across, weighs up to 10kg, and smells like rotting meat, attracting the carrion flies that act as pollinating agents. It lasts only a few days after blooming. Boardwalks lead from the park's information center to known *Rafflesia* habitats, but seeing a fully developed flower is a matter of luck. It is best to telephone park headquarters to find out if any are in bloom.

GUNUNG MULU NATIONAL PARK ✪✪✪

The most spectacular of Sarawak's natural wonders lies on the flanks of the 2,736m-peak of Gunung Mulu, 100km east of Miri. Here a thick band of limestone conceals a cave system which includes the world's largest cave – the 700m by 400m Sarawak Chamber, discovered in 1980. It ranges in height from 70m to over 110m. Deer Cave, about an hour's walk from park headquarters, has a huge colony of bats, which emerge in a swirling cloud each evening around dusk. A 10-minute boat trip leads to Clearwater Cave, which has a

plank-walk alongside the underground river leading to impressive limestone formations. A boardwalk and lights make the cave accessible, but there is plenty for adventure cavers as well. Sarawak Chamber can only be visited on an organized adventure caving trip. Mulu's pristine, diverse rainforest ecosystems can be experienced on a three-day trek to The Pinnacles, a "forest" of razor-sharp, 50m limestone pinnacles, or a four-day hike to the summit of Gunung Mulu and back, or an overnight hike on the Headhunter's Trail to Limbang in the north. The park deserves at least three days. A range of accommodation is available. Book at the Parks office or with tour agencies in Miri or Kuching.

MIRI ✪

Oil money gave Miri its brashness, tourism is refining it. The site of Malaysia's first oil well and offshore rigs, oil workers on leave and weekenders from Brunei give the city a lively air. It offers many good restaurants and an attractive beach, but most travelers use it as a base for exploring the Niah Caves and Gunung Mulu national parks.

NIAH NATIONAL PARK (➤ 26, TOP TEN)

National Parks and Wildlife Office

✉ Visitors' Information Centre, Kuching (➤ 82)

🔁 Miri (➤ 89), Niah Caves (➤ 26), Bario (➤ 87)

✈ Regular flights to Miri, Kuching and Brunei

➕ 83C3
Visitors' Information Centre
✉ 452 Jalan Melayu
☎ (085) 434181
🕐 Mon–Thu 8–4:15, Fri 8–4:45, Sat 8–12:45. Closed Sun

Dayak paintings on show at the Cultural Village

National Parks and Wildlife Office
☒ 32 Cross Road, Sibu
☎ (084) 340980
☒ Regular flights from Kuching to Sibu, Kapit and Belagai

RAJANG RIVER SAFARIS ✪✪✪

For centuries the Rajang River and its tributaries have served as a natural highway into the interior of Sarawak. Overland travel is difficult in this land of dense jungle, mountain and swamp, and boats have always been the major form of transport, from the traditional canoes of the native people (now propelled by outboard motors) to the seagoing coasters that trade upriver as far as Sibu. Regular ferries ply from Sibu upstream to Kapit, the starting point for expeditions to Iban and Orang Ulu longhouses. Permits are required and logistics are difficult, so it is best to take an organized tour. These generally depart from Sibu, and last from two to four days.

✚ 82A1
☒ 32km south of Kuching
🕐 Daily 8–4:30. Orang-utan feeding times: 8:30–9, 2:30–3
🚌 Bus 6 from Kuching
♿ None
 Free

SEMENGGOH ORANG-UTAN ✪✪
REHABILITATION CENTRE

This 740-hectare forest reserve is Sarawak's equivalent of the famous Sepilok Orang-Utan Sanctuary in Sabah. Here orang-utan, honey-bears, hornbills and other native animals which have been orphaned, injured, or recovered from poachers are nursed back to health and prepared for a return to the wild. You can watch the semi-wild orang-utan enjoy their daily feed in a tropical forest setting. Permits should be obtained at the Visitors' Centre in Kuching. There is a similar set-up in Matang Wildlife Centre, 20km west of Kuching. .

✚ 82B1
☒ 135km east of Kuching
🚌 Regular buses from Kuching and Sibu

SKRANG ✪✪✪

The most accessible and best set-up longhouse experience is along the Skrang and Lemanak Rivers, near Bandar Sri Aman. The Iban here have been receiving visitors for two decades and, while it might seem commercialized, the experience is civilized, yet interesting enough and comes complete with an excellent river journey. Tour agencies also run their own longhouse resorts here. Book through agencies in Kuching.

Where To...

Above: *Pulau Kapas*
Right: *Khoo Kongsi*

Peninsular Malaysia

Prices
Prices are approximate, based on a three-course meal for one without drinks and service:
$ = under RM15
$$ = RM15–40
$$$ = over RM40

Hawker Cuisine
Some of the tastiest food in Malaysia can be enjoyed at a hawker center: a gathering of dozens of tiny cooking stands, each specializing in a single dish. Choose a seat at the communal tables, then wander around the stands and order a selection of dishes; the cooks will be only too happy to explain the ingredients and preparation. You pay each cook separately when the food arrives at your table; other hawkers will come to take orders for drinks.

Kuala Lumpur

Bangles ($$)
An Indian restaurant with ambiance specializing in the Moghul cuisine of northern India.
✉ **60 Jalan Tuanku Abdul Rahman** ☎ **(03) 298 6770**
🕐 **Lunch, dinner**

Be Be's ($$)
Light, gourmet meals that are an innovative blend of East and West.
✉ **Hotel Capitol, Jalan Bukit Bintang** ☎ **(03) 243 7000**
🕐 **Lunch, dinner**

Bintang Walk ($–$$$)
Trendy people-watching promenade lined with sidewalk cafés, international restaurants and gourmet coffeehouses. There is also a Planet Hollywoood.
✉ **Jalan Bukit Bintang**
🕐 **Lunch, dinner**

Bon Ton ($$$)
Popular restaurant set in a converted bungalow serving Nyonya and Malay fare with a Western twist.
✉ **7 Jalan Kia Peng**
☎ **(03) 241 3614**
🕐 **Lunch, dinner**

Brickfields ($)
Excellent 'banana leaf' rice, Indian rice and curries, as well as breads. Near YMCA and Jalan Travers.
✉ **Jalan Tun Sambanthan, Brickfields** ☎ **(03) 273 3140**
🕐 **Breakfast, lunch, dinner**

Central Market ($–$$)
Two floors of the market building have restaurants and hawker stands offering Malay, Chinese and Indian specialties.
✉ **Jalan Hang Kasturi**
🕐 **10AM–10PM**

Chinatown ($)
Many good Chinese eateries, from hawker stands selling one-dish meals to restaurants serving morning dim-sum or wok-fried dishes to go with rice for dinner.
✉ **Jalan Petaling and surrounding roads**
🕐 **All day. Closes 2AM**

Coliseum Café ($–$$)
Faded relic of old-time Kuala Lumpur, with lively bar. Famous for its sizzling steaks. European and Asian cuisine.
✉ **Coliseum Hotel, 98–100 Jalan Tuanku Abdul Rahman**
☎ **(03) 292 6270**
🕐 **Lunch, dinner**

Hard Rock Café ($$$)
American burgers, steaks and loud rock music. Queues on weekends.
✉ **Concorde Hotel, 2 Jalan Sultan Ismail** ☎ **(03) 244 4062**
🕐 **Lunch, dinner**

Jalan Alor ($)
You can find excellent Chinese noodle dishes, chicken rice and grilled fish (*ikan bakar*) in Jalan Alor behind the Sungai Wang Hotel. Sit near the stands from which you order food.
✉ **Jalan Alor**
🕐 **7PM till late**

Kampung Baru ($)
Best Malay food in town, including regional favorites. The Pasar Minggu (Sunday Market), which takes place on Saturday night, is especially lively.
✉ **Jalan Raja Muda Musai**
🕐 **Breakfast, lunch, dinner**

Kapitan's Club ($$)
Atmospheric restaurant set in a restored Chinese

clanhouse, and specializing in Peranakan cuisine.

 35 Jalan Ampang
☎ (03) 201 0242
🕐 Lunch, dinner

Le Coq d'Or ($$)
Local and international cuisine, served in the palatial setting of an old colonial mansion once owned by a tin millionaire.
✉ 121 Jalan Ampang
☎ (03) 242 9732
🕐 Lunch, dinner

Nelayan Floating Restaurant ($$)
A picturesque, *kampung*-style restaurant set on a lakeside, offering a selection of Chinese, Malay and seafood dishes.
✉ Taman Tasik Titiwangsa, Jalan Temerloh (off Jalan Pahang) ☎ (03) 4022 8400
🕐 Lunch, dinner

Old China Cafe ($$)
Dine on Nyonya favorites. In this former Chinese laundry association some of the antiques are for sale.
✉ 11 Jalan Balai Polis
☎ (03) 232 5915
🕐 Lunch, dinner

Rasa Utara ($$)
Malay dishes from the Kedah region, in the comfort of an air-conditioned restaurant. Branches throughout Asia.
✉ Bukit Bintang Plaza, Jalan Bukit Bintang ☎ (03) 248 8369
🕐 Lunch, dinner

Sakura Satay Station ($$)
Upmarket, air-conditioned alternative to the traditional hawker centers, with a range of hawker specialties.
✉ 165 Jalan Imbi
☎ (03) 242 2319
🕐 Lunch, dinner

Scalini's ($$$)
Trendy, elegant Italian restaurant, set in the heart of the city's Golden Triangle.
✉ 19 Jalan Sultan Ismail
☎ (03) 245 3211
🕐 Lunch, dinner

Seri Melayu ($$)
Traditional Malay cuisine, accompanied by performances of traditional music and dance.
 1 Jalan Conlay
☎ (03) 241 4699
🕐 Dinner

Shang Palace ($$$)
One of Kuala Lumpur's top Chinese restaurants, with luxurious dining room and superb food. Noted for its *dim sum*.
✉ Shangri-La Hotel, Jalan Sultan Ismail ☎ (03) 232 2388
🕐 Lunch, dinner

The Taj ($$$)
Superb North Indian breads and biryani meals in a lovely setting. Live music at times.
✉ Crown Princess Hotel, Jalan Tun Razak ☎ (03) 2162 5522
🕐 Lunch, dinner

Teochew Restaurant ($$)
An excellent Chinese restaurant which serves Teochew specialties such as pork and fish concoctions.
✉ 270–272 Jalan Cangkat Thambi Dollah (off Jalan Pudu)
☎ (03) 241 5851
🕐 Lunch, dinner

TGI Friday's ($$)
American-style grill, part of the well-known chain, serving steaks, burgers, pizza and pasta. Branches throughout Malaysia.
✉ Life Centre, 99–100 Jalan Sultan Ismail ☎ (03) 263 7761
🕐 Lunch, dinner

Tasty Treats
Local cakes referred to as *kuih* are a favorite snack. There is an enormous variety of sweet and savory *kuih* available at roadside stands and hotel high-tea buffets. Other popular treats include *goreng pisang* (banana fritters), *vadeh* (Indian dhal doughnut), and curry puffs (deep-fried pastry with curried potato and sometimes meat or even sardine filling).

Big Ones, Small Ones...
Coconut is a staple ingredient of Malaysian cuisine. Its milk cools and complements fiery curries, sweetens desserts and adds fragrance to "sticky rice," or *nasi lemak*. The juice and flesh of young coconut provide a sweet and refreshing drink.

Cameron Highlands
Orient ($)
Chinese restaurant. A good place to try out the local "steamboat" specialty.
✉ **Jalan Besar Tanah Rata**
🕐 **Lunch, dinner**

Thanam ($)
An Indian restaurant with outdoor tables, serving a tasty menu of various curries, claypot rice and *murtabak*.
✉ **Jalan Besar, Tanah Rata**
🕐 **Lunch, dinner**

Smokehouse Hotel ($$$)
Excellent steaks in a cosy restaurant, cream teas in living-rooms or the garden; totally English, of course.
✉ **2km beyond Tanah Rata**
☎ **(05) 491 1215**
🕐 **Lunch, dinner**

Desaru
Seafood buffs should head for Sungai Rengit, a tiny town 26km south of Desaru, for fresh fish, prawns, oysters and crabs cooked Chinese style.
✉ **Sungai Rengit, Johor**
🕐 **Lunch, dinner**

Ipoh
Kedai Kopi Kong Meng ($)
Excellent selection of Ipoh Chinese hawker fare, including the famous chicken *kway teow* noodles, and the sour-spicy Turf Club *laksa* noodles.
✉ **Jalan Bandar Timah**
🕐 **Breakfast, lunch**

Ming Court ($$)
Queues form from dawn at this well-known *dim sum* dumpling restaurant. The customers can't be wrong!
✉ **Jalan Leong Sin Nam (near Excelsior Hotel)** 🕐 **Breakfast**

Restaurant Yum Yum ($$)
Good Nyonya and Chinese dishes, particularly fish and chicken, together with a warm ambience. This road is packed with eateries.
✉ **5 Persiaran Green Hill (near Excelsior Hotel)**
☎ **(05) 253 7686**
🕐 **Lunch, dinner**

Kota Bharu
Kow Lun ($$)
Among the best of the Chinese coffeeshops along this row. Hearty rice and meat and veg dishes as well as ice-cold beer.
✉ **7005 Jalan Kebun**
🕐 **Lunch, dinner**

Pasar Besar (Central Market) ($)
A good place to try the state's specialties of *nasi kunyit* and *nasi dagang*, a glutinous rice with curry, and Malay *kuih* (cakes).
✉ **Jalan Tengku Chik**
🕐 **Breakfast, lunch**

Pasar Malam (night market) ($)
Hawker stands offer a wide range of dishes, including local specialties such as the Thai-influenced *ayam percik* (barbecued chicken with green curry sauce), *keropok batang* (fish sausages served with chilli dipping sauce) and *nasi kerabu* (colored rice served with coconut and seaweed).
✉ **Jalan Padang Garong**
🕐 **Dinner**

Kuala Terengganu
Afzal Tandoori ($$)
Indian restaurant dishing up classic curries, *biryanis* and delicious nan bread, plus a few less common offerings such as fried quail.

27 Jalan Sultan Mahmud
☎ (09) 623 2913
🕐 Breakfast, lunch, dinner

Batu Buruk Food Centre ($)
Malay food stands under a covered pavilion at the southern end of the city beach. Try the local specialty *nasi padang*.
✉ Jalan Persinggahan
(off Jalan Sultan Mahmud)
🕐 Breakfast, lunch, dinner

Good Luck ($$)
Commonly called Lucky Restaurant, this typical Chinese eatery serves a wide range of Cantonese fare.
✉ 11 Jalan Kota Lama
☎ (09) 622 7573
🕐 Lunch, dinner

Kuantan
Riverside Hawker Centre ($)
A selection of outdoor stands serving a range of seafood and Malay specialities, and set on a pleasant riverbank.
✉ Jalan Besar 🕐 Dinner

Pak Pu Seafood Restaurant ($$)
Popular Chinese restaurant about 20 minutes from Kuantan, famous for stuffed crab and fish and lobster dishes. Windy, sea-facing tables, air-conditioned section.
✉ 6th Mile, Kuantan–Beserah Road 🕐 Lunch, dinner

Marang
Marang Guest House and Restaurant ($)
An attractive terrace restaurant with a wonderful view over the palm-fringed lagoon to the island of Kapas.
✉ Main Street, Marang
☎ (09) 618 9176
🕐 Lunch, dinner

Melaka
Banana Leaf ($)
Southern Indian vegetarian meals, beautifully presented on a banana-leaf 'plate.'
✉ 42 Jalan Munshi Abdullah
☎ (06) 283 2607
🕐 Breakfast, lunch, dinner

Glutton's Corner ($)
Long-established hawker center serving an interesting range of Malay, Chinese and Indian fare, including excellent *roti canai* breakfasts, and spicy beef and chicken satay.
✉ Jalan Taman Merdeka
🕐 Breakfast, lunch, dinner

Hoe Kee Chicken Rice ($)
Melaka's most famous chicken rice, cooked Hainanese style and served with billiard-sized balls of rice.
✉ 4 Jalan Hang Jebat
🕐 Lunch

Iguana Riverfront Restaurant ($$)
Trendy eatery fronting the river, with great ambience, and a wide and affordable selection of Melakan-and Western dishes and international beers.
✉ 15–17 Jalan Laksamana
☎ (06) 282 7440
🕐 Lunch, dinner

Heeren House ($$)
Attractive café in a small hotel overlooking Melaka River. Portuguese, Peranakan and Western cuisine and lovely cakes.
✉ 1 Jalan Tun Tan Cheng Lock
☎ (06) 281 4241
🕐 Breakfast, lunch, dinner

Madame Fatso's Restoran ($$)
Hawker-style set-up in a row of eateries. Famed for its

Fruity Treats
A bewildering variety of seasonal tropical fruits can be enjoyed in Malaysia, from bananas, pineapples and mangoes to more exotic delights such as starfruit (yellow, crisp and refreshing), rambutan (small red and "hairy," concealing a pale flesh that tastes like lychee), and durian (the "king of fruits," huge, green and spiky, with what many find to be a foul-smelling flesh that is definitely an acquired taste).

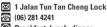

Combined Cultures

Peranakan means "born here" and refers to the descendants of the 19th-century Chinese in the British Straits Settlement states of Melaka, Penang and Singapore, who married local Malays. The cultural blend is particularly evident today in Peranakan (or Baba-Nyonya) cuisine, which combines Chinese ingredients and cooking techniques with Malay spices and flavorings, such as coconut and lemon grass, to produce tasty, intriguing results.

baked crab and "cook-it-yourself" steamboat.

✉ **Bunga Raya Glutton's Square, Jalan Merdeka (opposite Mahkota Parade)**
🕓 **Lunch, dinner**

Makhota Parade Food Centre ($)

Air-conditioned, indoor alternative to Glutton's Corner in a vast shopping center that also houses Western fast-food outlets, including big names like McDonalds, Dunkin' Donuts, A&W, and Burger King.

✉ **Jalan Taman Merdeka**
🕓 **Lunch, dinner**

Manis Sayang ($$)

Bright and busy Peranakan restaurant, which offers a wide-ranging menu.

✉ **617–618 Taman Melaka Raya** 🕾 **(06) 281 3393**
🕓 **Lunch, dinner**

Ole Sayang ($$)

Authentic Peranakan restaurant complete with restored traditional décor.

✉ **199 Jalan Taman Melaka Raya** 🕾 **(06) 283 1366**
🕓 **Lunch, dinner**

Peranakan ($$)

Opulent Peranakan villa with a garden courtyard serving delicious Peranakan dishes. Cultural shows are presented in the evenings. There is an equally attractive branch on Jalan Tun Tan Cheng Lock.

✉ **317C Jalan Klebang Besar (7km north on road to Port Dickson)** 🕾 **(06) 385 4436**
🕓 **Lunch, dinner**

Restoran de Lisbon ($)

Fresh seafood cooked Portuguese/Malay style in open courtyard. Live music every evening.

✉ **Medan Portugis (3km east of city center)**
🕾 **(06) 284 8067** 🕓 **Dinner**

Pulau Langkawi
Beach Garden Resort ($$)

Excellent European food, including steaks, waffles and coffee, and great margaritas in a lovely indoor or beach-side setting.

✉ **Pantai Cenang**
🕾 **(04) 955 1363**
🕓 **Breakfast, lunch, dinner**

Barn Thai ($$)

Good Thai food in an unusual setting in the middle of a mangrove forest; live jazz is sometimes performed.

✉ **Kampung Belangga Pecah**
🕾 **(04) 966 1001**
🕓 **Breakfast, lunch, dinner**

Champor-Champor ($$)

Elegant eating place offering a mix of Malay and European cuisine.

✉ **Pantai Cenang** 🕾 **(04) 955 1449** 🕓 **Lunch, dinner**

Prawn Village ($$)

Seafood cooked Cantonese style, with fresh crab and prawn specialties.

✉ **7 Persiaran Putra, Kuah**
🕾 **(04) 966 6111**
🕓 **Lunch, dinner**

Sari Seafood Village ($$)

Set on stilts over the water, good sunset views to go with Malay fare.

✉ **Persiaran Putra, Kuah**
🕾 **(04) 966 6192**
🕓 **Lunch, dinner**

Pulau Pinang (Penang)
Chowrasta Nasi Kandar stands ($$)

Arguably the best Indian-Muslim food in town if you can bear the surroundings.

Serving super-spicy curries with rice.

✉ **Jalan Chowrasta**
🕐 **Lunch, dinner**

Dawood ($$)
Established in 1947, Dawood serves authentic South Indian cuisine and traditional non-alcoholic Indian drinks such as the yogurt-based *lassi.*

✉ **63 Lebuh Queen, Georgetown** ☎ **(04) 261 1633**
🕐 **Lunch, dinner**

Eliza Malay Restaurant ($$)
Kampung-style buffets with live traditional Malay music at night. Good views of Georgetown.

✉ **City Bayview Hotel, Lebuh Farquar** ☎ **(04) 263 3161**
🕐 **Breakfast, lunch, dinner**

Gurney Drive hawker center ($)
Outdoor tables are set out next to the waterfront, with stands offering dishes such as satay, *char kway teow,* *laksa, nasi ayam, sotong* (cuttlefish), as well as numerous other traditional favorites.

✉ **Pesiaran Gurney, Bagan Jermal** 🕐 **Dinner**

Hot Wok Café ($$)
Old-style coffeeshop fitted out with marble tables and antiques, serving traditional Pinang and Nyonya dishes such as curry *kapitan* (delicious, spicy chicken curry), and *otak-otak.*

✉ **125D Jalan Tanjung Tokong, Desa Tanjung**
☎ **(04) 899 0858**
🕐 **Lunch, dinner**

Il Ritrovo ($$$)
Cosy Italian restaurant with a good range of pasta and pizzas served with international wines.

✉ **Casurina Beach Hotel, Tanjung Bungah** ☎ **(04) 8851 1171** 🕐 **Dinner**

Kurumaya ($$)
This Japanese restaurant has a relaxed atmosphere, and offers dishes such as *yakitori, teppanyaki, sashimi* and *sushi.*

✉ **269 Jalan Burma, Georgetown** ☎ **(04) 228 3222**
🕐 **Lunch, dinner**

Pulau Tikus hawker stands ($)
This inexpensive alternative to the Gurney Drive stands offers all the famous Penang goodies.

✉ **Pulau Tikus Market, Jalan Pasar** 🕐 **Breakfast, lunch, dinner**

Tandoori House ($$)
Authentic Moghul curry dishes from northern India are served up in an air-conditioned dining room.

✉ **36 Lorong Hutton, Georgetown** ☎ **(04) 261 9105**
🕐 **Lunch, dinner**

Tower Palace ($$$)
Expensive but good quality Chinese restaurant at the top of the Komtar Tower. Enjoy the superb views over Georgetown.

✉ **60th Floor, Komtar Tower, Kompleks Tuanku Abdul Razak, Jalan Pinang** ☎ **(04) 262 2222**
🕐 **Lunch, dinner**

The Bungalow ($$)
Old-world setting with sea views and a mix of dishes from steaks to Hainanese chicken rice.

✉ **Lone Pine Hotel**
☎ **(04) 881 1511**
🕐 **Breakfast, lunch, dinner**

Juices
Fruit juice is an ideal way to quench a tropical thirst, and can be bought, freshly squeezed, or in cans, from street stands and hawker centers. Lime, orange, papaya, guava and starfruit juice are all popular, but you will also see sugar-cane syrup (a sweet, green syrup extracted using a hand-cranked mangle) and soya-bean milk.

East Malaysia

Longhouse food
Sampling native cooking in the interiors of Sabah and Sarawak is an unforgettable experience. Although canned food is common, traditional favorites remain: fragrant hill rice served with barbecued wild-boar or fish, steamed riverbank ferns and bamboo shoots and occasionally exotica such as snake or monkey.

Kota Kinabalu

Nan Xing ($–$$)
A pleasant Chinese restaurant specializing in Cantonese cuisine, including *dim-sum*, as well as steaks and chops.
✉ 33–35 Jalan Haji Saman
☎ (088) 212900
🕐 Lunch, dinner

New Arafat ($)
Basic eatery serving Indian Muslim food, including delicious *roti canai* breakfasts.
✉ Block I, Sinsuran Kompleks, Jalan Pasar Baru 🕐 24 hours

Peppino ($$$)
Good Italian fare with a selection of wines and live Filipino music.
✉ Tanjung Aru Resort, Tanjung Aru ☎ (088) 225800
🕐 Lunch, dinner

Phoenix Court ($$$)
Stylish and expensive Chinese restaurant offering Cantonese and Szechuan specialties.
✉ Hyatt Kinabalu International, Jalan Datuk Salleh Sulong ☎ (088) 221234
🕐 Lunch, dinner

Port View ($–$$)
Lively, late-night seafood spot opposite the old Customs wharf. Choose your fish from one of the tanks.
✉ Jalan Haji Saman
☎ (088) 221753

Shiraz ($$)
Kota Kinabalu's top Indian restaurant, which specializes in spicy but not-too-hot Moghul curries and *biryanis*.
✉ Lot 5, Block B, Sedco Kompleks, Jalan Sapuloh
☎ (088) 225088
🕐 Lunch, dinner

Sri Kapitol Coffeehouse ($–$$)
Good Malay and Western specialties in this pleasant coffeeshop. Restaurant upstairs.
✉ Hotel Capital, 23 Jalan Haji Saman ☎ (088) 219688
🕐 Breakfast, lunch, dinner

Sri Melaka ($)
Excellent value restaurant with delicious Malay and Peranakan food.
✉ 9 Jalan Laiman Diki, Kampung Ayer ☎ (088) 55136
🕐 Breakfast, lunch, dinner

Tanjung Aru Hawker Centre ($)
A range of hawker stands set up along the city beach, serving mostly seafood dishes and traditional Malay specialities.
✉ Tanjung Aru beach
🕐 Dinner

Kuching

Chinese Food Centre ($)
Chinese selection of noodles and rice. Wash it down with ice-cold beer or fruit juice. More stalls on Jalan Wayang/Jalan Temple.
✉ Jalan Wayang (opposite temple) 🕐 Lunch, dinner

City Tower ($$)
Gourmet Chinese restaurant at the top of the Civic Centre tower, with superb views over the city. Cheaper meals and snacks are on offer here, but there are similarly good views in the neighboring cafeteria.
✉ Civic Centre, Jalan Budaya
☎ (082) 234396
🕐 Lunch, dinner

Dulit Coffee House ($–$$)
Attractive terrace café serving Western and local

WHERE TO EAT & DRINK

dishes, including excellent
kebabs and burgers

📧 **Telang Usan Hotel, Jalan
Ban Hock** ☎ (082) 415588
🕐 Breakfast, lunch, dinner

Green Vegetarian ($)
A very basic Indian
restaurant serving South
Indian vegetarian curries.
📧 **16 Main Bazaar**
🕐 Breakfast, lunch, dinner

Hani's Distro (£ ££)
Good value Asian and
Western food in a relaxed
bistro atmosphere.
📧 **Jalan Chan Chin Ann**
☎ (082) 245793
🕐 Lunch, dinner

Hornbill's Corner Cafe ($$)
BBQ steamboat in the
restaurant, televised English
Premier League and cold
beer at the bar. There is also
a value-for-money buffet.
📧 **Jalan Ban Hock**
☎ (082) 252 670 🕐 Lunch,
dinner

Lok Thian ($$)
Excellent Thai cuisine served
on the ground floor, gourmet
Chinese cuisine upstairs.
📧 **Bangunan Beesan, Jalan
Padungan** ☎ (082) 331310
🕐 Lunch, dinner

Open Air Market ($)
Rather misleading name for
a covered hawker center,
serving a wide range of tasty
Chinese and Malay dishes.
📧 **Jalan Market**
🕐 Lunch, dinner

San Francisco Grill ($$)
Pleasant steak restaurant
with a local touch; live piano
music in the evenings.
📧 **7B Jalan Ban Hock**
☎ (082) 258050
🕐 Lunch, dinner

See Good ($$)
This is the city's top Chinese
seafood restaurant. Choose
your own lobster, crab,
squid, prawns, and clams,
and have them cooked to
your particular taste.
📧 **Wisma Si Kiong, Jalan
Bukit Mata (behind MAS
offices)** ☎ (082) 232609
🕐 Lunch, dinner

Sri Sarawak ($$$)
Gourmet Malay and
European cuisine and
seafood, in a restaurant with
superb views over the river.
📧 **Riverside Majestic Hotel,
Jalan Tuanku Abdul Rahman**
☎ (082) 247777
🕐 Lunch, dinner

Top Spot Food Court ($)
Open-air hawker center set
on the roof of a multi-story
car park, with a huge array of
Chinese, Malay, and Indian
food stands. Good seafood.
📧 **Jalan Bukit Mata (behind
MAS offices)** 🕐 Lunch, dinner

Sandakan
Apollo ($$$)
This popular restaurant
serves tasty Chinese
seafood. This stretch has
several good eateries.
📧 **394 Jalan Yu Seng, Selatan
(near Gloria Hotel)** ☎ (085)
420813 🕐 Lunch, dinner

Ascanika Restoran ($)
Good roti (breads), Indian
curries and Indonesian
dishes.
📧 **Jalan China**
🕐 Breakfast, lunch, dinner

Malay Food Stalls ($)
Simple, tasty Malay fare,
including rice, noodles, and
satay.
📧 **Jalan China (near Hock Hua
Bank)** 🕐 Lunch, dinner

Vegetarian Food
Vegetarians are reasonably
well catered for in most
large Malaysian towns and
cities, where specialist
Indian (and occasionally
Chinese) vegetarian
restaurants can be found.
Elsewhere, it is more
difficult to avoid meat.
Vegans would do well to
request the omission of
eggs and seafood,
especially in soups. The
Malay for "I eat only
vegetables" is *saya hanya
makan sayur*.

Peninsular Malaysia

Prices
Prices are for a double room, excluding breakfast:
$ = under RM60
$$ = RM60–160
$$$ = over RM160

Story-teller's Bar
Kuala Lumpur's crumbling Coliseum Hotel is a relic of the days of British author Somerset Maugham, who once frequented the bar. Although faded and a little the worse for wear, the bar is full of character, still patronized by a noisy, mixed crowd of Chinese businessmen, journalists, local store-owners and curious travelers.

Kuala Lumpur

Backpackers Travellers Inn ($)
An established budget hotel in central Chinatown with dorms and air-conditioned rooms. Washing and cooking allowed.
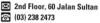 2nd Floor, 60 Jalan Sultan
☎ (03) 238 2473

Carcosa Seri Negara ($$$)
Luxury hotel in an elegantly restored colonial mansion set in beautiful gardens, the former residence and guest-house of the British resident Sir Frank Swettenham. Suites only.
✉ Persiaran Mahameru, Taman Tasik Perdana
☎ (03) 282 1888

Chamtan ($$)
Good-value air-conditioned rooms, each with telephone and private bath. Well-located in the heart of colorful Masjid India.
✉ 62 Jalan Masjid India
☎ (03) 293 0144

Coliseum ($)
Old and faded, but quiet, clean and good value, with a convenient central location. Try the famous restaurant and bar on the ground floor.
✉ 100 Jalan Tuanku Abdul Rahman ☎ (03) 292 6270

Heritage Station Hotel ($$)
This historic hotel is part of Kuala Lumpur's magnificent Moorish-style railway station building. Restored, it retains its colonial grace.
✉ Railway Station, Jalan Sultan Hishamuddin
☎ (03) 2273 5588

Hotel Capitol ($$)
Smack in the middle of Bukit Bintang. Uninspiring lobby, but good rooms, excellent restaurant and wines.
✉ Jalan Bukit Bintang
☎ (03) 243 7000

Katari ($$)
Friendly, clean hotel opposite Pudu Raya Bus Station with small rooms. Left luggage service.
✉ 38 Jalan Pudu
☎ (03) 201 7777

Mandarin Oriental ($$$)
Luxury hotel next to Petronas Twin Towers with command-ing views, six restaurants. It also has apartments.
✉ Kuala Lumpur City Center
☎ (03) 380 8888

Shangri-La ($$$)
Glamorous luxury hotel in the heart of the Golden Triangle, near shopping centers, bars, restaurants and businesses.
✉ 11 Jalan Sultan Ismail
☎ (03) 232 2388

Swiss Inn ($$)
Another good value Chinatown hotel, handy to Jalan Petaling night market, and with a good coffeeshop.
 62 Jalan Sultan ☎ (03) 232 3333

Vistana ($$)
Modern luxury hotel with reasonable prices located near Putra World Trade Centre. All rooms have air-conditioning, TV, bathroom and mini-bar. Restaurants, pool, travel agency and airport limo service.
✉ 9 Jalan Lumut (off Jalan Ipoh) ☎ (03) 442 8000

Cameron Highlands

Bala's Holiday Chalets ($)
Accommodations range from dormitory beds to

comfortable chalets equipped with private baths. Pleasant gardens with good views of the countryside.
✉ **Tanah Rata** ☎ (05) 491 1660

Smokehouse Hotel ($$$)
Beautifully renovated, "olde English" hotel with low ceilings, open log fires and a rose garden. Established 1937. Suites only.
✉ **Tanah Rata** ☎ (05) 491 1215

Ipoh
Casuarina ($$$)
Large luxury hotel 10 minutes from the airport, with a swimming pool, spa, disco, and restaurants. Good views from rooms.
✉ **18 Jalan Gopeng** ☎ (05) 255 5555

Majestic ($$)
Colonial station hotel built in the early 1900s, and modernized in the 1990s. The better rooms have private verandahs, polished wooden floors, and rattan furniture.
✉ **Railway Station, Jalan Club** ☎ (05) 255 5605

Kota Bharu
Juita Inn ($$)
Central, clean and good value for money. Air-conditioned restaurant attached.
✉ **Jalan Ping-Pong** ☎ (09) 744 6888

Perdana ($$$)
The best hotel in town, equipped with luxury rooms, good restaurant, swimming pool, tennis court and car park. Convenient location close to museum and cultural center.
✉ **Jalan Mahmud** ☎ (09) 778 5000

Perdana Resort ($$)
Some chalets overlook a lovely beach. Good restaurants.
✉ **Pantai Cahaya** ☎ (09) 733 3000

Melaka
Heeren House ($$)
Beautifully converted warehouse beside Melaka River, with polished wood floors and antique furniture.
✉ **1 Jalan Tun Tan Cheng Lok** ☎ (06) 281 4241

Majestic ($)
A rambling old colonial-style hotel that has certainly seen better days, but nevertheless still offers a taste of faded elegance at budget prices.
✉ **188 Jalan Bunga Raya** ☎ (06) 282 2455

Hotel Puri ($$)
Beautifully restored Peranakan manor in the historical center, with modern rooms, a café and gardens.
✉ **118, Jalan Tn Tan Cheng Lock** ☎ (06) 282 5588

Ramada Renaissance ($$$)
Melaka's top luxury hotel, with roof-top swimming pool, tennis and squash courts, disco, and several restaurants.
✉ **Jalan Bendahara** ☎ (06) 284 8888

Pulau Langkawi
Beach Garden ($$)
Good value German-run beach hotel with swimming pool. Air-conditioning and ensuite bathrooms.
✉ **Pantai Cenang** ☎ (04) 955 1363

Pelangi Beach Resort ($$$)
One of the island's most luxurious resorts, with Malay

Hotel Taxes
A 5 per cent tax is charged on all hotel bills in Malaysia. In the more expensive hotels a further 10 per cent service charge is added. The taxes apply to bigger restaurants, too, but are not reflected in menu prices.

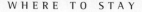

Preserving Heritage
Tourism is a major incentive to preserve heritage architecture. Penang, Melaka, Terengganu and the hill stations have some prime examples of 19th-century shophouses and bungalows that have been restored and renovated for use as boutique and budget accommodation. Many beach and rainforest chalet resorts draw inspiration from the traditional wooden Malay house.

chalets spread throughout landscaped gardens.
✉ **Pantai Cenang**
☎ **(04) 955 1001**

Pulau Pangkor
Pangkor Laut Resort ($$$)
Exclusive resort on private island off Pangkor's west coast. Luxury villas plus pool, tennis courts, night-club, and beautiful beaches.
✉ **Pulau Pangkor Laut**
☎ **(05) 699 1100**

Sri Bayu Beach Resort ($$)
Charming resort with chalets arranged in *kampung*-style, in gardens. Open-air restaurant and disco.
✉ **Jalan Pasir Bogak, Pulau Pangkor** ☎ **(05) 685 1929**

Pulau Pinang (Penang)
Baba's Guest House ($)
Friendly, family-run guesthouse offering dormitory beds and air-conditioned rooms with private bath.
✉ **Batu Feringghi**
☎ **(04) 881 1686**

Cathay Hotel ($)
A central, well-run hotel with character. Restaurant at the back.
✉ **15 Lebuh Leith**
☎ **(04) 262 6271**

Copthorne Orchid ($$)
Situated on a private beachfront with a fine view of Tanjung Bungah bay, this is one of the nearest hotels to Georgetown and the airport. Most of the 318 rooms and suites overlook the bay. Excellent restaurants and sports and leisure facilities, plus a good business center.
✉ **Tanjung Bungah**
☎ **(04) 890 3333**

Lone Pine Hotel ($$)
The first tourist lodge of Feringghi beach is now a charming boutique hotel run by the famous E&O hotel group. Pre-war and 1970s furnishings, a beautiful restaurant and a long beachfront.
✉ **97 Batu Feringghi**
☎ **(04) 881 1511**

Rasa Sayang ($$$)
Arguably Penang's most famous beach hotel, Rasa Sayang has luxurious rooms, good restaurants and lots of character. The excellent pool is surrounded by landscaped gardens.
✉ **Batu Feringghi**
☎ **(04) 881 1811**

Sunway Hotel ($$)
Convenient to shops and restaurants, with city and sea views.
✉ **33 New Lane**
☎ **(04) 229 9988**

Pulau Tioman
Berjaya Imperial Beach Resort ($$$)
Well-run luxury resort, with air-conditioned chalets set in hillside gardens above one of Tioman's most beautiful beaches. Facilities include watersports, golf, tennis and horse-riding.
✉ **Pulau Tioman**
☎ **(09) 414 5445**

Taman Negara
Taman Negara Resort ($–$$$)
Luxury lodge with a range of rooms from air-conditioned chalets to dorms and campsites.
✉ **Park HQ, Kuala Tahan**
☎ **(09) 266 3500, (03) 245 5585 (Kuala Lumpur)**

East Malaysia

Kota Kinabalu

Backpackers Lodge ($)
Comfortable dormitory beds designed for the budget traveler, with shared bathroom, common room and laundry facilities.
✉ **25 Lorong Dewan, Australia Place** ☎ **(088) 261495**

City Inn ($–$$)
Central, good value, clean and popular. Book ahead.
✉ **41 Jalan Pantai**
☎ **(088) 218933**

Jesselton ($$$)
Kota Kinabalu's oldest hotel, which was founded in 1954, has been renovated to provide all modern facilities, but still exudes colonial charm and elegance.
✉ **69 Jalan Gaya**
☎ **(088) 223333**

Tanjung Aru Resort ($$$)
Sabah's top luxury beach resort, run by Shangri-La. Attractive, landscaped gardens have been laid out beside a beautiful palm-fringed beach. Swimming pools, tennis courts, pitch-and-putt, watersports, sailing, and scuba diving are among its many facilities.
✉ **Tanjung Aru**
☎ **(088) 225800**

Kuching

Anglican Guesthouse ($)
Pleasant, spacious budget rooms atop a hill with a pretty garden.
✉ **Behind St Thomas' Cathedral (pedestrians enter from Jalan Carpenter, vehicles from Jalan McDougall)**
☎ **(082) 414027**

Borneo ($$)
This is Kuching's longest established hotel, and offers large, attractive rooms and attentive service.
✉ **30 Jalan Tabuan**
☎ **(082) 244122**

Kuching Hilton ($$$)
Luxury hotel overlooking the river with a nice pool and a good steakhouse. Its sister hotel, the Hilton Batang Ai Longhouse Resort, is a lakeside jungle resort 275km east of Kuching.
✉ **Jalan Tuanku Abdul Rahman** ☎ **(082) 248200**

Telang Usan ($$)
Friendly hotel, run by Orang Ulu people, with lovely traditional native décor. Good eateries and crafts shop.
✉ **Jalan Ban Hock**
☎ **(082) 415588**

Kundasang

Perkasa ($$)
Luxury hotel near Mount Kinabalu, with superb panoramic views of the mountain. Facilities include tennis court, restaurant and cocktail bar. Transport to national park is provided.
✉ **Kundasang, Sabah**
☎ **(000) 214142**

Miri

Holiday Inn ($$$)
Popular hotel at the river mouth, set in a pleasantly landscaped garden. Pretty sunsets over the sea.
✉ **Jalan Temenggong Datuk Oyong Lawai** ☎ **(085) 418888**

Sandakan

London ($)
Clean and efficient budget hotel offering modest air-conditioned rooms with private bath. The central location is a plus.
✉ **Block 10, Jalan Empat**
☎ **(089) 216371**

Desert Islands
Travelers who really want to get away from it all can find solitude on Malaysia's islands such as Sabah's Tunku Abdul Rahman Park and Terengganu's Perhentian. Though bigger resorts are muscling in, there are still stretches with basic beach huts or chalets, and no phones, TV or air conditioning. You live on the beach, eat at a little seaside café, and retire to your hut only to sleep.

Handicraft & Antique Stores

Batik and *Songket*
Malaysia is famous for the beautiful fabrics known as batik and *songket*. Batik, of Javanese origins, is made by painting patterns on cotton or silk using liquid wax, and dyeing the cloth several times to build up attractive designs. *Songket* is a delicate and expensive brocade made by interweaving colored silk with threads of silver and gold.

Peninsular Malaysia

Kuala Lumpur
Aseanea
A gallery specializing in Asean crafts in the basement of Suria Kuala Lumpur City Centre (KLCC) under Petronas Twin Towers. Sells chinoiserie, clothing, jewelry, and homewares.
✉ **Suria KLCC**

Kompleks Budaya Kraf (Craft Cultural Complex)
A massive complex of souvenir shops selling (and demonstrating) things Malaysian, including batik, pottery and textiles.
✉ **Kompleks Budaya Kraf, Jalan Conlay** ☎ **(03) 2164 4344**

Masjid India
Colorful Indian and Muslim quarter with *songkok*, silk saris, cotton *kurta* outfits, bangles, and incense.
✉ **Jalan Masjid India**

Royal Selangor
Homegrown multinational with beautiful pewter artifacts, from vases and bowls to tankards and chess sets.
✉ **4 Jalan Usahawan Enam, Setapak Jaya** ☎ **(03) 4022 1000**

Kota Bharu
Pantai Cahaya Bulan
The 5km road from Kota Bharu to PCB is dotted with workshops producing Kelantan's famous Malay handicrafts, including kites, batik, silk, and *songket*.
✉ **Jalan Pantai Cahaya Bulan**

Sultanah Zainab
This street has many shops selling Kelantan silver worked into souvenirs, filigree jewelry, and betelnut boxes.

Mainly family businesses like KB Permai.
✉ **Jalan Sultanah Zainab**

Kuala Terengganu
Chendering
An area with large handicraft stores: Kraftangan Malaysia specializes in brass and *songket*, Noor Arfa Batek and the Suterasemai Silk Centre in batik and silk respectively.
✉ **Chendering (7km south of Kuala Terengganu)**

Jalan Bandar
A Chinatown street that has been invaded by souvenir outlets such as Teratai at No. 151. Good but expensive arts and crafts are available. The Batik Gallery at No.192 offers trendy batik designs and fashions.
✉ **Jalan Bandar**

Melaka
Adventure Art-Craft
Native regional woodcraft objects such as masks and statuesusing a mix of old and modern designs.
✉ **60 Jalan Tokong**
☎ **(06) 317 1793**

Earth Collections
Charming outlet with arty, innovative souvenirs and knick-knacks, including clogs, pottery, and woodwork.
✉ **62 Jalan Tun Tan Cheng Lock** ☎ **(06) 317 1793**

Jonkers Street
Also known as Jalan Hang Jebat, this Chinatown street has long been the center of Melaka's famous antiques trade. The streets around here are full of fascinating shops selling artifacts and souvenirs. Shop around!
✉ **Jalan Hang Jebat**

Orang-Utan House
Malaysian souvenirs, T-shirts and art pieces featuring the bright colors and tongue-in-cheek signature of artist-owner Charles Cham.
✉ 59 Lorong Hang Jebat, Chinatown ☎ (06) 282 6872

Pulau Langkawi
Kompleks Budaya Kraf
Handicrafts contor that encompasses a craft museum and cultural theater, plus outlets for Royal Selangor pewter, Karyaneka, Batek Malaysia and other craft shops.
✉ Block B, Teluk Yu, Mukim Bohor (15 minutes' drive from the airport) ☎ (04) 959 1913

Pulau Pinang (Penang)
Komtar
The Kompleks Tunku Abdul Rahman houses a labyrinth of stores, restaurants, and two department stores.
✉ Jalan Penang, Georgetown

Little India
This tiny area has stores packed with colorful saris and Indian cottons and silks, jewelry and spices.
✉ Jalan Mesjid Kapitan Keling

Hong Giap Hang
Atmospheric old Chinese shophouse whose recesses are stacked with antiques and traditional furniture. Try also Saw Joo Aun (139 Jalan Pintai Tali).
✉ Jalan Penang (opposite Police HQ)

Craft Batik
Batik apparel, household items, and souvenirs. The factory is open to visitors.
✉ Teluk Bahang
☎ (04) 885 1302

Yahong Art Gallery
Owned by Chuah Thean Teng, the father of Malaysian batik art. Art gallery upstairs, antiques in basement; also souvenirs.
✉ 58D Batu Feringghi
☎ (04) 881 1251

East Malaysia

Kuching
Main Bazaar
This row of shops boasts the gamut of Bornean and Asian antiques and handicrafts. Wood carvings, beadwork, basketry, and Iban *pua kumbu* textiles come in all shades of authenticity and innovation. Notable outlets include Fabriko (No. 20), Sarakraf (No. 34) and Thian Seng (No. 48).
✉ Main Bazaar (opposite the waterfront)

Mohamed Yahia & Sons
Probably the best bookstores in town, with a great selection of maps and historical and natural history literature on Borneo.
✉ Holiday Inn ☎ (082) 254282
✉ Sarawak Plaza ☎ 416928

Jalan Carpenter
This street, the main axis of Kuching's Chinatown, is lined at its western end with dozens of goldsmiths' shops.
✉ Jalan Carpenter

Sarawak Crafts and Art Bazaar
Sarawak Craft Council event featuring handicrafts and demonstrations, including beadwork, pottery and art, all of which are on sale. First Saturday of each month.
✉ Waterfront
☎ (082) 312381

The *Kris*
The *kris* is the traditional Malay dagger, with a distinctive wavy blade and an ornately decorated pistol-grip hilt. It has long been a symbol of honor, and was presented to young men to mark the passage from youth to manhood. The iron blade always has an odd number of waves, and the hilt, made of wood or ivory, is usually carved in the design of a bird's head. Antiques older than 1850 cannot be exported without a license from Museum authorities.

Markets

Night Markets

The *pasar malam*, or "night market," is a Malaysian institution found in towns and cities all over the country. Generally beginning around dusk and continuing into the small hours, the setup of itinerant stands combines the functions of shopping, eating and entertainment, with music from CDs of Western, Chinese and Malay rock bands, and mouth-watering hawker food alongside fresh produce and clothing.

Peninsular Malaysia

Kuala Lumpur

Chow Kit

KL's largest street market, where local people swarm along the pavements and alleys looking for cheap clothes and shoes, fresh produce, traditional medicines, music cassettes and CDs, and much more. Beware of pickpockets and bag-snatchers here.

📧 **Jalan Haji Hussein (off Jalan Tuanku Abdul Rahman)** ⏰ **Daily 10–5**

Jalan Petaling

The main axis of Kuala Lumpur's Chinatown is a busy crush of street-stands and barrows selling everything from "designer" T-shirts and pirated CDs and videos, to Nepalese jewelry and copy watches.

📧 **Jalan Petaling** ⏰ **Daily 5PM–10PM**

Jalan TAR Pasar Malam

On Saturday nights the length of Jalan TAR is closed to vehicles and transformed into a bright and noisy night market. Musicians entertain the crowds thronging among stands that are piled high with cheap clothes, food and drink.

📧 **Jalan Tuanku Abdul Rahman** ⏰ **7PM–2AM**

Pasar Minggu (Sunday Market)

Kampung Bahru's "Sunday market" actually begins on Saturday night and runs into the early hours of Sunday. It is a treasure-trove of Malay and Islamic wares such as *songkok* (fez), pottery and other handicrafts, textiles, and Arabic calligraphy.

📧 **Jalan Raja Muda Musa, Kampung Baru** ⏰ **Sat 6PM–2AM**

Pasar Seni (Central Market)

This 1930s Art Deco building once housed the city's wet market, but is now given over to dozens of stands and shops selling souvenirs, hats, clothes, bags, basketry, rattan, batik, kites, and all kinds of other handicrafts. Also has exhibitions and cultural performances.

📧 **Jalan Hang Kasturi** ☎ **(03) 2274 6542** ⏰ **Daily 10AM–10PM**

Pudu Market

This is one of the city's biggest and busiest wet markets, where you can make your choice from a mind-boggling variety of tropical fruits and vegetables, fresh seafood and anything from a deep-fried duck's foot to a side of pork. Make sure you bring your camera.

📧 **Jalan Pasar Baru (2km southeast of city center)** ⏰ **Mon–Sat 8–4**

Kota Bharu

Pasar Besar (Central Market)

This colorful market is housed in an octagonal, concrete building, and the traders are mainly women in their bright clothing. The wet section is downstairs, where fresh produce is sold. Upstairs are the dry goods and food sections and, on the upper floors, Malay handicrafts such as cotton sarongs and silverwork.

📧 **Jalan Hulu** ⏰ **Daily 9–5**

Kuala Terengganu

Pasar Besar (Central Market)

A modern, multi-story building overlooking the

waterfront houses a lively market, which is well worth a look. There's a wet market on the ground floor, while the stands on the upper floors include several good craft shops selling excellent batik, *songket*, brassware and other handicrafts and souvenirs.

✉ **Jalan Bandar** 🕐 **Daily 8AM–9PM**

Melaka
Souvenir Market
A small collection of souvenir stands lines a lane that leads from near A Famosa down to Glutton's Corner, but the quality of goods on sale here is generally rather poor. A better option would be to save your money for the antique shops in Jalan Hang Jebat (also known as Jonkers Street ➤ 104).

✉ **Between Jalan Kota and Jalan Taman Merdeka** 🕐 **Daily 9–9**

Pulau Pinang (Penang)
Batu Feringghi
The main street in Batu Feringghi comes alive in the evenings with market stands selling souvenirs, batik, jewelry, T-shirts, drinks, and snacks.

✉ **Batu Feringghi** 🕐 **Daily 6PM–1AM**

Chowrasta Market
One of Penang's oldest markets, the wet section is a noisy morning affair. Upstairs are bales of cotton and silk, while the shops facing Penang Road are bursting with dried and preserved nutmeg and mango – local specialties.

✉ **Jalan Pintal Tali (off Lebuh Campbell)** 🕐 **Daily 9–6**

East Malaysia
Kota Kinabalu
Filipino Market
A two-story building on the waterfront houses a lively market run mainly by Filipino immigrants. Stands aimed mainly at tourists sell hand-made baskets, sea shells, souvenirs, and tribal artifacts from Sabah.

✉ **Jalan Tun Fuad Stephens** 🕐 **Daily 8AM–9PM**

Jalan Gaya
On Sunday mornings Jalan Gaya comes alive with a bustle of market stands selling all manner of goods, ranging from fruit, flowers and vegetables to pets, souvenirs and handicrafts.

✉ **Jalan Gaya** 🕐 **Sun 7–1**

Kuching
Pasar Minggu (Sunday Market)
A colorful weekly bazaar where the natives from the outskirts gather to sell their farm vegetables, along with produce such as wild honey, orchid plants and jungle fruit. There are good handicrafts stalls here, too, and excellent hawker food. The market is at its liveliest on Saturday night and early Sunday morning. Keep a grip on your belongings.

✉ **Jalan Satok, at junction with Jalan Palm (1km southwest of city center)** 🕐 **Sat 2PM–Sun 12PM**

Wet Market
The waterfront of the west end of Jalan Gambier is lined with crowded stands selling fresh fish, meat, fruit, and vegetables.

✉ **Jalan Gambier** 🕐 **Daily 9–6**

Haggling
Unless you're in a department store, bargain when buying anything, from fruit to souvenirs. Never buy at the first shop. Offer less than you're prepared to pay then haggle until you settle on an acceptable figure. Smile and keep the proceedings good-natured, and never make a firm offer unless you truly intend to buy.

Shopping Centers

Shopping in Comfort

Malaysia's countless modern shopping malls provide a comfortable, air-conditioned shopping environment. Although there are bargains to be had, KL cannot compete with Singapore when it comes to choice and cheap electronic equipment. The best deals will be found on sports gear, watches, jewelry, CDs, videos, apparel and handicraft. Most shopping centers open daily 10AM–10PM.

Peninsular Malaysia

Kuala Lumpur

Imbi Plaza

This small shopping center, on the southern edge of the Golden Triangle, specializes in high-quality computers, computer accessories, and peripherals. The plaza offers a mind-boggling variety of inexpensive software and CD-ROMs.

✉ **Jalan Imbi**

Mid Valley Megamall

In line with Malaysia's "bigger is better" axiom, this five-level, 400-store center is among Asia's largest. The anchor tenants – Jaya Jusco, Carrefour, and Metrojaya department stores – offer a huge range of foods and products, some of which are exclusive. There are also many specialty stores, themed restaurants, and movie theaters.

✉ **Mid Valley**

Star Hill Shopping Centre

The CK Tang department store is the anchor for this collection of designer boutiques housed in airy colonnades around a curved atrium. Some famous names whose clothes are featured here include Anne Klein, Bally, Ferragamo, Dunhill, Cerruti 1881, and Dolce e Gabbano.

✉ **Jalan Bukit Bintang**

Sungei Wang Plaza

Located in Kuala Lumpur's Bukit Bintang shopping district and surrounded by malls, this is one of the city's most popular centers. Together with the neighboring Bukit Bintang Plaza, Sungei Wang Plaza is built around the Parkson-Grand and Metrojaya superstores, and is strong on bargain electronic and electrical goods, sports gear, photographic equipment, clothes, and footwear. There is also a vast selection of sweet and candy stalls, and plenty of Asian and Western fast food outlets.

✉ **Jalan Sultan Ismail and Jalan Bukit Bintang**

Suria KLCC

Overlooking a 20-hectare landscaped park, this fashionable, well-designed mall at the base of the Petronas Twin Towers has a good blend of stores, including Asiana, gifts, branded goods, and kids' products, as well as movie theaters and excellent international restaurants.

✉ **76 Jalan Raja Culan**

The Mall

The shops here are based around the Japanese Aktif Lifestyle department store. There is also a fun park, complete with dodgems and carousels for the kids. On the top floor is a Melaka-themed hawker center.

✉ **100 Jalan Putra**

The Weld

An upmarket mall with expensive shops, Chinese and Western fast-food restaurants, a Delifrance café in the atrium and a Times bookshop upstairs.

✉ **76 Jalan Raja Culan**

Johor Bahru

Plaza Kota Raya

This popular shopping center, with five floors of retailers, includes a supermarket and department store, many inexpensive clothing and footwear outlets, and several fast-food joints.

✉ **Jalan Tebrau**

Melaka
Makhota Parade

This vast shopping mall was built on reclaimed land on Melaka's waterfront, and features a basement supermarket plus three levels of shops, covering just about everything imaginable: furniture, electronics, photographic equipment, jewelry, sports goods, and toys. There are also several fast-food outlets, a food court and, a bowling alley, a movie theater, and an MPH bookstore.

✉ **Jalan Taman Merdeka**

Pulau Pinang
Komtar

Short for "Kompleks Tuanku Adbul Razak," the Komtar's 65-story tower is a major local landmark. The center houses a labyrinth of little stores, restaurants, cafés, and amusement arcades, plus two large department stores. There is also a small Times bookstore on an upper level of the Aktif Lifestyle department store. Located at the end of Jalan Penang, a busy shopping street, Komtar is near the batik, antique, and local goods stores of old Chinatown.

✉ **Jalan Penang, Georgetown**

East Malaysia

Kota Kinabalu
Centre Point

Anchored by the Aktif Lifestyle department store, this is the biggest of Kota Kinabalu's many shopping centers. There are a few good handicraft stores – look for Borneo Handicraft and Ceramic Shop on the ground floor in particular – and take a look in the bookstore upstairs in Aktif Lifestyle.

✉ **Jalan Pasar Baru**

Wisma Merdeka

A low-rise labyrinth of stores and fast-food restaurants at the northern end of the city center. Borneo Handicraft upstairs has a good selection of handicrafts, while Borneo Books has a good choice of books about the natural history and the indigenous peoples of Sabah.

✉ **Jalan Haji Saman and Jalan Lima Belas**

Kuching
Riverside Complex

A pleasant, air-conditioned plaza across the way from the Holiday Inn hotel, with a supermarket, a department store and, upstairs, a Times bookstore, a great place to browse through an excellent range of English-language books. The mall lies at the east end of Kuching's attractive waterfront, not far from Main Bazaar and Jalan Carpenter.

✉ **Jalan Tunku Abdul Rahman**

Sarawak Plaza

This sprawling mall stretches east from the Holiday Inn and contains various shops selling Hong Kong-inspired apparel, local and Asian souvenirs, and an interesting assortment of other products. A good selection of books on Sarawak can be found at Mohamed Yahia, in the basement, and there is the usual range of fast-food eateries.

✉ **Jalan Abell**

Kites

Kite-flying was introduced to Malaysia from China, and has been a traditional pastime since the days of the 15th-century Melaka sultanate. Malay kites, called *wau*, are still hand-made in Kelantan, and are popular as souvenirs. They are made of brightly colored paper or cloth stretched over bamboo frames in various shapes.

Children's Attractions

Orang-Utans
The orang-utan sanctuaries at Sepilok, Sabah (▶ 78) and Semenggok, Sarawak (▶ 90) give children the magical experience of being able to see these remarkable creatures at close quarters, when the young apes get their daily meal of bananas at special feeding platforms in the jungle. Remember that the orang-utans of Sepilok and Semenggoh are wild animals, and no matter how cute they look they can be aggressive, throwing dung and sticks at anyone who gets too close. They are very curious, however, and seem to be attracted by brightly colored objects. A group of young apes at Sepilok once became so enamored of one unfortunate tourist's clothes that they stripped him naked!

Peninsular Malaysia

Kuala Lumpur
Batik Classes
Kids will enjoy coming up with their own batik creations using wax and dyes at the Kuala Lumpur Craft Complex. Instruction and materials are included.
✉ **Jalan Conlay** ☎ **(03) 2162 7459** ⏰ **Daily 9–5**

Butterfly Farm (▶ 38)

Menara KL (KL Tower) (▶ 35)

Mines Wonderland
Theme park set in beautifully landscaped remains of open-cast tin mine. Range of white-knuckle rides plus Snow House, Animal Kingdom, Musical Fountain and nightly laser show.
✉ **Jalan Sungai Besi, 20 minutes south of KL** ☎ **(03) 942 5010** ⏰ **Daily 4PM–11PM** 🍴 **Restaurant and snack bars ($$)** 💰 **Expensive**

Petrosains Museum
This offers an interactive, fun-filled experience based on the oil and gas industry. Attractions include giant molecules and 'time travel.'
✉ **Level 4, KLCC** ☎ **(03) 581 8181** ⏰ **Daily 9:30–5:30, Fri 2:30–7, Mon closed**

Sunway Lagoon
Popular theme park with a wave pool, water rides, and "Wild West" area. Next door, Sunway Pyramid mall has an ice-skating rink and a movie theater.
✉ **Bandar Sunway, Petaling Jaya** ☎ **(03) 735 6000** ⏰ **Mon–Fri 12PM –7:30; Sat, Sun, pub hols 10AM–7:30PM Closed Tue** 🍴 **Fast food** 💰 **Expensive**

Zoo Negara (▶ 69)

Desaru (▶ 40)
Clean, pleasant family beach resort area. All hotels have water sports facilities. There is a water theme park at Desaru Impian Resort.
✉ **90km east of Johor Bahru**

Langkawi
Underwater World
Over 100 tanks are home to 5000 fish, invertebrates, corals and other marine life. Observe the underbellies of leopard shark and manta rays in a walk-through tank.
✉ **Pantai Cenang** ☎ **(04) 955 6100** ⏰ **Daily 10–7:30**

Melaka
Crocodile Farm
Malaysia's largest crocodile farm rears more than 100 varieties of crocodile, including albinos. Feeding times are the biggest attraction.
✉ **Ayer Keroh (▶ 40)** ⏰ **Daily 9–6** 💰 **Inexpensive**

A Famosa Water World
A water theme park with various slides, a wave pool and a 500-meter-long river ride. This attraction is set in a golf resort which also offers horse-riding and watersports.
✉ **Alor Gajah** ⏰ **Mon–Fri 12–7:30, Sat, Sun, pub hols 9–8** 💰 **Moderate**

Melaka Zoo and Ayer Keroh Lake
Melaka's zoo is small but attractively landscaped, with a good selection of Malaysian wildlife. The nearby lake has paddle-boats and canoes for hire.
✉ **Ayer Keroh (▶ 40)** ⏰ **Daily 9–6** 💰 **Inexpensive**

Pahang
Club Med Cherating
Circus acts and supervised activities will keep children happy in this resort, which sprawls on a private beach. Nearby is a Turtle Information Centre with live turtles.
🖂 **Batu 29, Jalan Kuantan/ Kemaman, Cherating**
☎ **(09) 581 9133, (03) 261 4599**

Pulau Pinang (Penang)
Bukit Bendera (Penang Hill)
A trip on the funicular railway to the summit of Penang Hill (➤ 62) is interesting and has the added attraction of a playground at the top, as well as hiking trails, and a little zoo near the hotel.
🖂 **Ayer Hitam, 6km west of Georgetown** 🚃 **Trains daily every 30 mins, 6:30AM–9:30PM**
🖐 **Inexpensive**

Butterfly Farm (➤ 62)

Muka Head
Take a fishing boat from Teluk Bahang fishing village to this pleasant swimming beach. There is also a lighthouse at Muka Head, which can be reached on foot through well-marked rainforest trails.
🖂 **Teluk Bahang**

East Malaysia

Kinarut
Horse-riding
South of Kota Kinabalu, an Australian guide leads leisurely trail rides through villages or along the beach on good-tempered horses.
🖂 **Kindawan Riding Centre**
☎ **(088) 225 525** 🚃 **6:30–10, 3–6**

Kuching
Cat Museum
A small museum dedicated to the cat and its history, and featuring displays of cat memorabilia. A delight for cat lovers.
🖂 **Kuching North City Hall**
🚃 **Tue–Sun 9–5**

Matung Wildlife Centre
A chance to see native animals such as orang-utan, honey bear and hornbills in natural surroundings. Boardwalks, trails, picnic areas and waterfall.
🖂 **30km west of Kuching**
🚃 **Daily 8–5:30**
🖐 **Inexpensive**

Kota Kinabalu

Rafflesia Information Centre
The world's largest flower is celebrated in this informative and well thought-out center. The lucky might get to see the rare parasite in full bloom in the forest reserve behind the center.
🖂 **Kota Kinabalu/Tambunan Road** ☎ **(087) 774 691**
🚃 **Mon–Fri 8:45–12:45, 2–5**

Train journey
The rail journey from Beaufort to Tenom, southwest of Kota Kinabalu, follows a scenic route through Padas Gorge (➤ 76). You can make the trip on the tiny railcar (air-conditioned, with just 13 seats) in an hour and a half, or two hours on a diesel train. For the best views, sit on the right-hand side (from Beaufort to Tenom).
🖂 **Booking Office: Tanjung Aru Station, Kota Kinabalu**
☎ **(088) 254611** 🚃 **Mon–Sat, three trains from Tanjung Aru–Beaufort–Tenom. Sun, one train from Tanjung Aru, three trains from Beaufort–Tenom**
🚌 **Minibus from Kota Kinabalu to Beaufort** 🖐 **Moderate**

The Heat Factor
Don't forget that young ones are especially vulnerable to the effects of the tropical sun. Take along plenty of sunscreen, see that they wear sun hats or baseball caps and are well covered from 11 to 3. Make sure that they drink plenty of fluids to avoid dehydration. Sunscreen is readily available at pharmacies and department stores.

111

Cultural Shows

Let's Dance
The most popular of Malaysia's traditional dances is the *joget*, performed during cultural celebrations and Malay wedding ceremonies. Men and women take part in the elaborate, fast-tempo dance, and although they weave in and out they never touch. The dance has Portuguese origins, and is better known in Melaka as the *cakuncak*.

Peninsular Malaysia

Kuala Lumpur
Central Market
Occasional *wayang kulit* shadow puppet shows and cultural dances. Check with the local tourist office.
✉ Jalan Hang Kasturi
☎ (03) 2274 6542 🕓 Evenings

Dewan Filharmonic Petronas
A professional dance troupe gives scheduled traditional performances. Check listings.
✉ Kuala Lumpur City Centre
☎ (03) 207 7007

Istana Budaya
The national theater offers occasional Malay, Chinese and Indian classical and contemporary drama, music or dance. Check dailies or call.
✉ Jalan Tun Razak (near Lake Titiwangsa) ☎ (03) 402 55932

Seri Melayu Restaurant
(➤ 93)

Kota Bharu
Gelanggang Seri
A good place to see traditional Malay pastimes such as top-spinning, *wau* (kite-flying), *silat* (self-defense), and *rebana ubi* (giant drum) sessions. Tourist Information Centre has schedules.
✉ Jalan Mahmud
☎ (09) 485534

Melaka
Medan Portugis
This 'village square' on the coast south of Melaka is the heart of the Portuguese community in the town. Diners at the Restoran de Lisbon (➤ 96) can enjoy live cultural shows on Saturdays.
✉ Medan Portugis
(3km east of city center)

Mini Malaysia
Cultural shows are staged daily at this heritage park at Ayer Keroh (➤ 40).
✉ Ayer Keroh (12km north of Melaka) ☎ (06) 232 3176
🕓 Daily 9–6

Pulau Pinang (Penang)
Istana Theatre-Restaurant
A banquet of classic Malay cuisine accompanied by a performance of traditional music and dance.
✉ Pinang Cultural Centre, 288 Jalan Teluk Bahang
☎ (04) 885 1175
🕓 Daily 6–10PM

East Malaysia

Kota Kinabalu
Pesta Kadmatan
During May, the indigenous peoples celebrate the Harvest Festival in colorful village and longhouse ceremonies. The largest celebration is the Pesta Kadmatan among the Kadazandusun people in Penampang (13km south of Kota Kinabalu).
✉ Hongkod Koisaan, Penampang 🕓 30 & 31 May

Kuching
Kampung Budaya Sarawak (Sarawak Cultural Village)
Short cultural demonstrations in each "house," plus two full concerts daily showcasing the music and dance of the various ethnic groups. There are special performances during the Gawai Harvest Festival in May/June, celebrated in Kuching with a Mardi Gras.
✉ Pantai Damai, Santubong
☎ (082) 846411
🕓 Daily 9–5:15 (concerts); 11:30 & 4:30 (dance performances)

Nightlife

Peninsular Malaysia

Kuala Lumpur

Backroom
The party begins at 11PM at this ultra-modern techno/jungle club.
✉ 8 Lorong P Ramlee
☎ (03) 381 2998 ⏰ Daily 9PM–4AM

El Nino
Popular Latin dance club in a converted bungalow with live band and beer garden. Spanish restaurant upstairs
✉ Jalan Mayang (off Jalan Yap Kwang Seng) ☎ (03) 2164 4995 ⏰ Daily 6PM–4AM (restaurant open 12PM–3PM, 6PM–10PM)

Emporium Grand Café
Trendy mix of Latin, jazz and dance music, live bands, and Mediterranean and local food.
✉ Corner Jalan Sultan Ismail/Jalan P. Ramlee ☎ (03) 242 6666 ⏰ Daily 12PM–2AM (Bands start 9–10PM)

Hard Rock Café
One of the liveliest nightspots in Kuala Lumpur, offering live bands and dance music.
✉ Concorde Hotel, 2 Jalan Sultan Ismail ☎ (03) 244 2200 ⏰ Daily 9PM–2AM (3AM Fri & Sat). Live bands begin 11PM

Modesto's
Pub chain with hip decor, hit music, and excellent pizzas.
✉ The Embassy, 28 Jalan Ampang ☎ (03) 2166 3460; also in Jalan P. Ramlee, Damansara Heights, and Bangsar) ⏰ Daily 12PM–3AM (Music from 10PM)

Melaka
Stardust Discotheque
Disco with the usual pop dance music spun by DJs.

The Utan Fun Pub in the same hotel has live bands.
✉ Renaissance Melaka Hotel, Jalan Bendahara ⏰ Disco Fri & Sat 6PM–2AM; Pub daily 6PM–1AM

Penang
20 Leith Street
Popular bar and bistro in a renovated shophouse where dance music is played late at night. A favorite with trendy locals and tourists.
✉ 20 Lebuh Leith, Georgetown ☎ (04) 261 8573 ⏰ Daily 6PM–2AM (Fri & Sat 3AM)

Penang
Beer's Pub
A friendly sports bar that features live bands and DJs, with pool, darts, soccer via satellite TV, and quirky decor including styrofoam cutouts and banknotes on the ceiling.
✉ Parkroyal Resort Batu Feringghi ☎ (04) 881 1133 ⏰ Daily 11AM–3AM

East Malaysia

Kota Kinabalu
Shennanigans
The top pub in town, where the in-crowd hang out. Good live band.
✉ Hyatt Kinabalu International ☎ (088) 221234 ⏰ Daily 6PM–2AM

Kuching
De Tavern
Cosy pub on the waterfront opposite the Hilton. Good for drinks and a chat.
✉ Jalan Tuanku Abdul Rahman ⏰ Daily 7PM–2AM

Jupiter
Hottest dance place in town, with a live band belting out top-of-the-pops and requests.
✉ Jalan Ban Hock ☎ (082) 248200 ⏰ Daily 10PM–3AM

The Place to Be
Besides the Golden Triangle, KL's other trendy nightspot is a suburb, 4km to the southwest. Middle-class Bangsar is cosmopolitan, with classy, expensive restaurants, stylish pubs and coffeehouses that come and go with the new moon, drawing young professional Malaysians and expatriates.

Sports

Sporting Malaysians
The government is keen to promote Malaysia's sporting profile. As well as hosting the Commonwealth Games in 1998, which resulted in the Bukit Jalil Sports Complex in KL, it has instituted many annual international events. Among them are the Tour de Langkawi cycle race and the Mount Kinabalu Climbathon. Malaysia is also on the World Motorcycle Grand Prix and the Formula One circuits. In 1997 it sponsored the first successful climb by Malaysians to the summit of Mount Everest.

Malaysians are keen about sports, and particularly enjoy soccer, badminton, tennis, squash, and hockey, as well as exciting regional sports such as *sepak takraw* (an enjoyable spectator sport requiring tremendous agility from the two teams kicking a small, hard, woven-rattan ball back and forth over a high net). Many Malaysians are fond of outdoor activities such as hiking, cycling, and scuba-diving. There is no shortage of opportunities for the holiday-maker who wants to indulge in a little sporting activity.

Fishing
Malaysia has excellent opportunities for fishing, ranging from big-game fishing for black marlin in the waters of the South China Sea to freshwater fishing in the lakes and rivers of the interior, where the famous *kelah* (a relative of the Indian *mahseer*) is generally considered to be the most challenging prey. Permits are required for anyone wanting to fish in national parks and marine parks.
Persutuan Memancing Malaysia (Malaysian Angler's Association) ☎ **(03) 738 8864**

Caving
Malaysia is one of the world's most interesting and challlenging countries for caving. Sarawak offers international-standard experiences in the Mulu area for both the novice and the spelunker, with some of the world's largest caves, fascinating formations that are still "growing," and lots of insect and animal life. In the Peninsula, there are caving opportunities at the Batu Caves in Selangor, and in the limestone hills around Perate and Perlis.
Mulu National Park ☎ **(085) 434561**
Malaysian Nature Society ☎ **(03) 287 9442**

Golf
Golf is very popular in Malaysia. Some of the more outstanding courses include:

Kuala Lumpur
Royal Selangor Golf Club
Founded in 1893, this is the second oldest club in the country. It offers two challenging championship courses, and is the venue for the Malaysian Open.
✉ **PO Box 11051, 50734 Kuala Lumpur** ☎ **(03) 984 8433**

Saujana Golf and Country Club
The most expensive and prestigious club in Malaysia, Saujana Golf and Country Club is one of the world's top 100 courses.
✉ **PO Box 610, 46770 Petaling Jaya** ☎ **(03) 746 1466**

Cameron Highlands
Cameron Highlands Golf Club
This charming but difficult course is laid out in a beautiful setting among the rainforest-clad hills. Founded as a five-hole course in 1935, it was extended to 18 holes in 1974.
✉ **15–16 Main Road, PO Box 25, 39007 Tanah Rata**
☎ **(05) 491 1154**

Kuching
Damai Beach Golf Course
This international-class golf course, designed by Arnold Palmer, lies in a dramatic and

beautiful location between the peak of Gunung Santubong and the South China Sea.

✉ **Jalan Santubong, PO Box 400, 93902 Kuching**
☎ **(082) 846088**

Pulau Pinang
Bukit Jambul Country Club

Designed by Robert Trent Jones, this is one of Malaysia's most scenically impressive golf courses, meandering among tropical fruit trees and rock outcrops.

✉ **2 Jalan Bukit Jambul, 11900 Bayan Lepas, Pinang**
☎ **(04) 644 2255**

Pulau Tioman
Tioman Island Golf Club

Set amid swaying palms above the turquoise waters of the South China Sea, this 18-hole, par 71 course offers lucky members the opportunity of golfing in paradise. The clubhouse overlooks the beach as well as the 18th green. The club is part of the Berjaya Imperial Beach Resort.

✉ **Pulau Tioman, PO Box 4, 86807 Mersing, Johor**
☎ **(09) 414 5445**

Hiking

Malaysia offers a wide variety of hiking trails through some of the world's most beautiful primary rainforest, rich in exotic flora and fauna. Treks range from a one-hour stroll to expeditions of several days. Marked trails are concentrated in national parks and forest reserves such as Taman Negara (➤ 22), Kinabalu (➤ 18), Gunung Mulu (➤ 88), Bako (➤ 87), Taman Alam Kuala Selangor (➤ 68), Cameron Highlands (➤ 25) and other

hill resorts. Inquire at the respective destinations or specialist adventure tour agencies.

Scuba-diving

The crystal clear waters of the South China Sea and Sulu Sea provide some of the finest diving in the world, the best being Sipadan, off Sabah. However, the islands off the Peninsula's east coast offer diversity and beauty. There is no lack of dive operators, whether on-site or in the cities, offering instruction, trips, and equipment rental and sales.

Malaysian Sport Diving Association ☎ **(03) 833 9939**

Watersports

There are plenty of facilities for dinghy sailing, wind-surfing, water-skiing, canoeing and a number of other water-based activities to be found at many of Malaysia's more popular beach resorts, including Pulau Langkawi, Pulau Pangkor, Pulau Tioman, Penang, Desaru, Santubong and Tanjung Aru. Dam resorts also offer these facilities, among them, Kenyir (Terengganu) and Pedu (Kedah).

White-water Rafting

Shooting the rapids in rafts and one- and two-person kayaks is popular at a number of sites, including the Padas River in Sabah, the Skrang River in Sarawak, the Tembeling River in Pahang and the Selangor River and Nenggiri River in Kelantan. Half- to several-day tours are available. Check local papers for listings.

Trekking

Trekking in Malaysia's national parks provides the opportunity to experience one of the world's most diverse ecosystems. The country boasts over 8,000 species of flowering plants, 200 of mammals, 450 of birds, 250 of reptiles and 150,000 of insects (with many more yet to be discovered). The national flower is the hibiscus (known locally as *bunga raya*) and the national butterfly is the Rajah Brooke birdwing, whose large black wings are adorned with a flash of iridescent green.

What's On When

Penitents' Pilgrimage

Thaipusam is the Hindu festival of penance that annually draws crowds of 100,000 pilgrims, devotees and on-lookers to the Batu Caves, outside Kuala Lumpur, and the Nattulcotai Chettiar temple in Penang. Devotees pray, fast and join the procession of Lord Muruga by carrying jugs of milk or *kavadis,* which are large, cage-like structures, decorated with flowers, feathers and religious images, borne on long spikes which pierce the bearers' flesh.

Malaysians celebrate numerous religious festivals that are based on the lunar or Muslim calendars, and so vary in time from year to year. Check with Tourism Malaysia for forthcoming events. The most celebrated festival is *Hari Raya Aidilfitri,* the Muslim festival celebrating the end of Ramadan, the month of fasting and abstinence. It is a two-day national holiday. Another Muslim festival is *Hari Raya Haji,* celebrating the annual pilgrimage to Mecca.

January/February

Thaipusam: Hindu festival when devotees pay homage to Lord Muruga (see panel).
Chinese New Year: 15-day festival celebrated by the Chinese with family reunions, feasting, and lion dances.
Johor Kite Festival: A colorful international event in which kites of all designs take to the skies of Pasir Gudang in Johor.

April

Easter: candle-lit processions from St. Peter's Church in Melaka on Palm Sunday.
Malaysian World Motorcycle Grand Prix: Shah Alam.

May

Wesak Day: celebrates the Buddha's birth, enlightenment and death, marked by ceremonies at Buddhist temples.
Pesta Keamatan: Harvest festival celebration with native ceremonies and cultural events, Kota Kinabalu.
International Kite Festival: Kota Bharu.
International Dragon Boat Festival: Penang.

Penang Bridge Run: Fun-filled event when runners, walkers, and families tackle the 13km-long bridge.

June

Gawai Dyak: Harvest festival celebration throughout Sarawak in the longhouses and a Mardi Gras through Kuching.
International Dragon Boat Race: Kota Kinabalu.
Pesta San Pedro: Portuguese fishermen's festival, Melaka.

August

Hari Kebangsaan: Malaysia's National Day, marked with parades through Kuala Lumpur.

September

Malaysia Fest: Month-long tourism event kicked off with a cultural parade, with special events, promotions and food fairs in hotels and shopping centers.
Lantern Festival: Georgetown Esplanade, Penang.

October

Mount Kinabalu International Climbathon: A race up Malaysia's highest mountain.

November

Deepavali: Hindu 'Festival of Light' celebrating the return from exile of Lord Rama, marked by fire-walking ceremonies at Hindu temples.

December

Christmas: celebrated with midnight mass and carolers
New Year's Eve: mass countdowns at town squares; a festive occasion, especially in Kuala Lumpur and Penang.

Practical Matters

Traveling and eating, Malaysia-style

TIME DIFFERENCES

GMT	Malaysia	Germany	USA (NY)	Netherlands	Spain
12 noon	8PM	1PM	7AM	1PM	1PM

BEFORE YOU GO

WHAT YOU NEED

● Required
○ Suggested
▲ Not required

	UK	Germany	USA	Netherlands	Spain
Passport/National Identity Card	●	●	●	●	●
Visa	▲	▲	▲	▲	▲
Onward or Return Ticket	●	●	●	●	●
Health Inoculations (Hepatitis A and B, Cholera, Polio, Tetanus, Typhoid)	○	○	○	○	○
Health Documentation (► 123, Health)	○	○	○	○	○
Travel Insurance	○	○	○	○	○
Driving License (International)	●	●	●	●	●
Car Insurance Certificate (if own car)	●	●	●	●	●
Car Registration Document (if own car)	●	●	●	●	●

WHEN TO GO

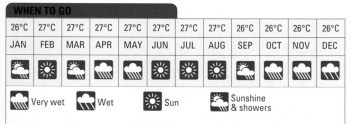

26°C	27°C	27°C	27°C	27°C	27°C	27°C	27°C	26°C	26°C	26°C	26°C
JAN	FEB	MAR	APR	MAY	JUN	JUL	AUG	SEP	OCT	NOV	DEC

Very wet Wet Sun Sunshine & showers

Average humidity: 70–90 per cent (higher in the rainy season)

TOURIST OFFICES

In the USA

Tourism Malaysia
595 Madison Avenue
Suite 1800
New York, NY 10022

☎ 212/754 1113/4/5/7
Fax: 212/754 1116
mtpb@aol.com

818, Suite 804
West 7th Street
Los Angeles, CA 90017

☎ 213/689 9702
Fax: 213/689 1530
info@tourismmalaysia.com

In Germany

Tourism Malaysia
Rossmarkt 11
60311 Frankfurt am Main

☎ 069 283 782
Fax: 069 282 215

In the UK

Tourism Malaysia
Malaysia House
57 Trafalgar Square
London WC2N 5DU

☎ 020 7930 7932
Fax: 020 7930 9015
info@malaysia.org.uk

POLICE 999

AMBULANCE 999

FIRE 994

WHEN YOU ARE THERE

ARRIVING

More than 50 international airlines fly to Kuala Lumpur (and some to Penang, Langkawi, Johor Bahru, Kuching, Kota Kinabalu and Labuan). Malaysia Airlines and British Airways are the main carriers from the UK – non-stop flight time is about 13 hours.

Kuala Lumpur International (or Sepang) Airport
International/domestic   **Journey times**

🚇	N/A
🚆	60 minutes
🚌	45 minutes

70 kilometers to city center

Sultan Abdul Aziz Shah (or Subang) Airport
Domestic only

   Journey times

🚇	60 minutes
🚆	30 minutes
🚌	20 minutes

24 kilometers to city center

MONEY

The unit of currency is the Malaysian ringgit (RM), unofficially called the dollar. It is divided into 100 sen. Coins are 1, 5, 10, 20 and 50 sen and 1 ringgit; banknotes are 1, 2, 5, 10, 20, 50, and 100 ringgit. The RM is pegged to the US$ at RM3.80 (1999) and is legal tender only in Malaysia. There are restrictions on how much may be taken out of the country; amounts must be declared at customs. Money can be exchanged, and travelers' checks cashed, at banks, money changers (the best rates), hotels, department stores, and shopping centers. Credit cards are widely accepted in cities.

TIME

 Malaysia is eight hours ahead of Greenwich Mean Time (GMT+8) throughout the year.

CUSTOMS

→ **YES**

Goods Obtained Duty Free (Limits for importation into Malaysia):
Alcohol: 1L
Cigarettes: 200 or
Cigars: 50 or
Tobacco: 225g
Souvenirs and gifts: not exceeding RM200. Amounts above these limits (plus carpets, garments, clothing accessories, jewelry, handbags and chocolates) are liable to duty. Visitors bringing in dutiable goods may have to pay a deposit for temporary importation (refundable on departure). Items such as cameras, video equipment, portable radio cassette players, cameras, watches, pens, lighters, perfumes and cosmetics do not attract duty. You must declare plants and animals or parts thereof, and taped video cassettes.

— **NO**

Drugs **(penalty: death)**, weapons (including imitations), fire crackers, counterfeit currency, pornography.

UK
(03) 248 2122
(Jalan Ampang)

Germany
(03) 242 9666
(Jalan U Thant)

USA
(03) 248 9011
(Jalan Tun Razak)

Netherlands
(03) 248 5151
(Jalan Mesra)

Spain
(03) 248 4868
(Jalan Ampang)

WHEN YOU ARE THERE

TOURISM MALAYSIA

Website:
http://tourism.gov.my

Head Office
● 17th Floor
  Menara Dato Onn
  Putra Trade Centre
  45 Jalan Tun Ismail
  50480 Kuala Lumpur
  ☎ (03) 2935188

Northern Region
● 10 Jalan Tun Syed Sheh
  Barakbah
  10200 Penang
  ☎ (04) 2619067

Southern Region
● Johor Tourist Information
  Centre, Jalan Ayer Molek
  80000 Johor Bahru
  ☎ (07) 2223591

East Coast Region
● 5th floor, Menara Yayasan
  Islam Terengganu
  Jalan Sultan Omar
  20300 Kuala Terengganu
  ☎ (09) 6221433

Sabah
● Ground Floor
  Bangunan EON CMG Life
  1 Jalan Sagunting
  88000 Kota Kinabalu
  ☎ (088) 248698

Sarawak
● 2nd Floor
  Bangunan Rugayah
  Jalan Song Thian Cheok
  93100 Kuching
  ☎ (082) 246575

NATIONAL HOLIDAYS

1 Jan	New Year's Day (except Johor, Kedah, Kelantan, Perlis, Terengganu)
Jan/Feb*	Chinese New Year
Jan/Feb*	Hari Raya Aidilfitri
Apr*	Hari Raya Haji
Apr/May	Awal Muharram (Muslim New Year)
1 May	Labour Day
May	Wesak Day
Jun (1st Sat)	The King's (Yang di-Pertuan Agong) Birthday
Jul*	Birthday of the Prophet Muhammad
31 Aug	National Day
Oct/Nov	Deepavali (except Sarawak and Sabah)
25 Dec	Christmas Day

* Holidays whose dates vary from year to year

OPENING HOURS

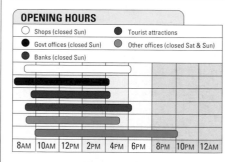

○ Shops (closed Sun)   ● Tourist attractions
● Govt offices (closed Sun)   ● Other offices (closed Sat & Sun)
● Banks (closed Sun)

8AM 10AM 12PM 2PM 4PM 6PM 8PM 10PM 12AM

Lunch is generally taken between 12:45–2, except Fridays when it is 12:45–2:45. The work week runs from Monday to Friday, except in Kelantan, Terengganu, Perlis and Kedah; these states observe the Muslim working week of Sunday to Thursday. Government offices are open half day Saturday (until 1PM) but close the first and third Saturday of the month. Similarly, banks are open half day Saturday (until 11:30AM), also closing the first and third Saturday of the month. Temples are open to visitors any time, but mosques are closed during prayers.

PUBLIC TRANSPORT

 Internal Flights Malaysia Airlines links Kuala Lumpur to all major cities and towns of the peninsula (an hour at most) and to East Malaysia (at least two hours). Other airlines, including Pelangi Air and Air Asia, service popular tourist destinations, including resort islands.

 Trains KTM Berhad provides a comfortable and economical service that goes from Singapore to Thailand along the west and east coasts of Peninsular Malaysia, with Kuala Lumpur as the hub. Express trains, stopping only at major towns, provide the best service for tourists.

 Long Distance Buses There are regular bus services to most parts of the country. Express (air-conditioned) buses connect all major towns. Tickets are cheap but services do not always run on time. Long-distance 'share' taxis also service all towns.

 Ferries No sea connection exists between the peninsula and East Malaysia. However, there are regular ferry services between the peninsula and its main islands, including Penang and Tioman. Express boat services operate in the interior of Sarawak and others serve coastal towns, including Labuan and Brunei.

 Urban Transport Kuala Lumpur is served by the fast KTM Komuter electric train, which goes out to the suburbs, plus the modern LRT (Light Rail Transit) system, which runs above ground through the city center. There are also buses and minibuses. Transport elsewhere is by bus.

CAR RENTAL

Many of the international car-hire companies have desks at airports, large hotels and major shopping and office complexes. There are also numerous local operators. You can normally pick a car up in one city and drop it off in another. You will need an international driving license. All cars have air-conditioning.

TAXIS

 Taxis can be hailed road-side, from taxi stands, or booked by phone. Only city cabs use meters. Elsewhere, agree a price beforehand. Surcharges apply for trips between midnight and 6AM; more than two passengers; luggage; and phone bookings. For airport and rail station taxis, buy coupons at the taxi desk.

DRIVING

 Speed limit on expressways and highways: **110kph**

 Speed limit on trunk roads: **80kph**

 Speed limit on urban roads: **50kph**

 The wearing of seat belts is compulsory, though belts are fitted to front seats only.

 There is random breath-testing. Limit: 0.08% blood/alcohol level.

 Petrol is inexpensive. Unleaded petrol is available and petrol stations are well distributed, especially in or near towns. They have toilets and sell drinks (important to prevent dehydration). Many open 24 hours a day ("*24 jam*") and take credit cards. Some stations in the cities are self-service.

If you break down in a rental car you should follow the instructions given in the documentation; most inter-national rental firms provide a rescue service. For a nominal fee, AA members can join the Automobile Association of Malaysia (AAM), 25 Jalan Yap Kwan Seng, Kuala Lumpur, ☎ (03) 2162 5777. Just bring your Automobile Association membership card.

PERSONAL SAFETY

Malaysia is relatively safe – violent crimes against tourists are rare. Pickpocketing and bag-snatching is a problem in some cities. If you need help, or lose an item of value, contact the English-speaking Tourist Police. They are distinguishable in the street by the checkered bands on their caps. For safety:

- Carry only what you need in a safe place on your person. Have your passport with you at all times.
- Leave valuables in your hotel deposit box.
- Do not take short cuts in deserted streets at night.

Police assistance:

 999 from any call box

TELEPHONES

Public telephones are coin- or card-operated. Coin phones can only be used to make calls within the country and require coins of 10, 20 and 50 sen and 1 ringgit. Card phones (*Kadfon*) can be used for local and international calls. Telekom cards are available from most retail outlets in values of 3, 5, 10, 20 and 50 ringgit. Some booths accept credit cards too.

International Dialling Codes

From Malaysia to:	
UK:	**00 44**
Germany:	**00 49**
USA:	**00 1**
Netherlands:	**00 31**
Spain:	**00 34**

COMMUNICATIONS

Post Offices
There are post offices in cities and most towns. They offer a range of services, including express mail and sometimes fax. Open 8–5 (1PM Sat); closed Sun (Fri: Kedah, Kelantan, Terengganu).
Internet access
There are many internet cafés, especially in shopping centers. Backpackers' hostels are usually equipped.

ELECTRICITY

The power supply in Malaysia is: 220–240 volts. Sockets accept three-square-pin (UK-style) plugs, although some older places have three-round-pin plugs. An adaptor is needed for Continental European appliances, and a voltage transformer for appliances operating on 100–120 volts.

TIPS/GRATUITIES

Yes ✓ No ✗		
Hotels (service included)	✗	
Restaurants (service included)	✓	change
Cafés (service included)	✗	
Taxis	✗	
Rickshaws	✗	
Tour guides	✓	10%
Porters	✓	RM2–5
Chambermaids	✓	RM2–5
Hairdressers	✗	
Toilets	✗	

HEALTH

Insurance

Malaysia has no reciprocal health agreements with other countries so medical insurance is essential. Medical treatment is available at government hospitals, specialist centers and private clinics. AEA/SOS International Assistance schemes cover Malaysia.

Dental Services

Dental treatment has to be paid for but private medical insurance will cover costs. If you have to pay for treatment make sure you keep all documentation to claim it back later.

Sun Advice

With temperatures that fluctuate little throughout the year (an average of 21–32°C) you can get sunburned at any time, but especially 11AM–3PM and by the sea. The tropical sun is deceptively strong. Wear a hat and use a high-factor sunscreen.

Drugs

You have the choice of pharmacies dispensing western medicines or "Chinese medical halls" selling traditional Chinese herbal medicines. They are often found in department stores and supermarkets and are well stocked for minor ailments.

Safe Water

Drink boiled water in major cities in Peninsular Malaysia. If you are unsure of hygiene standards in hawker centers, stay away from the ice. Bottled water is widely available. Remember to drink enough!

CONCESSIONS

Students/Youths Malaysia is appealing for youth and student travel because of its low cost of living and wide range of outdoor activities. Student and youth discounts are mostly confined to Malaysian nationals. An International Student Identity Card (ISIC) is of limited use but worth bringing as it can be useful at hostels; flashing it may sometimes bring discounts.
Senior Citizens Malaysia is not an obvious destination for older travelers; some find the equatorial climate and food difficult to cope with. There are, however, holidays specifically designed for senior citizens such as those offered by Saga Holidays, Saga Building, Middelburg Square, Folkestone, Kent CT20 1AZ, United Kingdom (☎ 0800 414383).

CLOTHING SIZES

Malaysia	UK	Rest of Europe	USA		
36	36	46	36		
38	38	48	38		
40	40	50	40		
42	42	52	42		Suits
44	44	54	44		
46	46	56	46		
7	7	41	8		
7.5	7.5	42	8.5		
8.5	8.5	43	9.5		
9.5	9.5	44	10.5		Shoes
10.5	10.5	45	11.5		
11	11	46	12		
14.5	14.5	37	14.5		
15	15	38	15		
15.5	15.5	39/40	15.5		Shirts
16	16	41	16		
16.5	16.5	42	16.5		
17	17	43	17		
8	8	34	6		
10	10	36	8		
12	12	38	10		
14	14	40	12		Dresses
16	16	42	14		
18	18	44	16		
4.5	4.5	38	6		
5	5	38	6.5		
5.5	5.5	39	7		
6	6	39	7.5		Shoes
6.5	6.5	40	8		
7	7	41	8.5		

WHEN DEPARTING

- On your arrival in Malaysia you complete a disembarkation form; the embarkation portion returned to you must be presented on your departure, including between the peninsula and Sabah and Sarawak; likewise with a currency declaration form.
- There is an airport departure tax of RM40 for international flights and RM5 for domestic flights payable at airline check-in desks.

LANGUAGE

Bahasa Malaysia is the official language of Malaysia, but as it is a multiracial country you will hear many languages. Bahasa Malaysia is a colourful mixture of many other tongues – including Sanskrit, Arabic and English. English is very widely spoken in the cities and, to an extent, in popular tourist destinations. Below are some words of Bahasa Malaysia you may find helpful.

hotel	*hotel*	fan	*kipas*
rest house	*rumah rehat*	hot water	*air panas*
dormitory	*rumah tumpangan*	bathroom	*bilik mandi*
room	*bilik*	toilet	*tandas*
..for one/two people	*..untuk satu/dua orang*	bed	*tempat katil*
		bed sheet	*cadar*
..for one/two nights	*..untuk satu/dua malam*	pillow	*bantal*
		sleep	*tidur*
air-conditioning	*air-con*	telephone	*telefon*

bank	*bank*	coin	*duit/wang syiling*
exchange office	*penukar matawang*	credit card	*kad kredit*
		traveller's cheque	*cek kembara*
post office	*pejabat*	exchange rate	*kadar tukaran asing*
foreign exchange	*tukaran matawang asing*	commission	*komisyen*
money	*wang/duit*	charge	
dollar	*ringgit*	how much?	*berapa harganya?*
cent	*sen*	expensive	*mahal*
banknote	*duit/wang kertas*	inexpensive	*murah*

restaurant	*restoran*	vegetables	*sayur-sayuran*
soup	*sup*	boiled rice	*nasi putih*
beef	*daging lembu*	fried rice	*nasi goreng*
pork	*babi*	fried noodles	*mee goreng*
chicken	*ayam*	hot (spicy)	*pedas*
fish	*ikan*	sweet (tasting)	*manis*
prawns	*udang*	cold	*sejuk*
egg	*telur*	drinks	*minuman*

aeroplane	*kapal terbang*	taxi	*teksi*
airport	*lapangan terbang*	car	*kereta*
train	*keretapi*	rickshaw/trishaw	*beca*
..station	*..stesen keretapi*	ticket	*tiket*
bus	*bas*	..single/return	*..satu hala/pergi balik*
..station	*..stesen bas*	..first/second class	*..kelas satu*
boat	*bot*	.. economy class	*..kelas ekonomi*
..port	*..pelabuhan*		

yes	*ya*	sorry	*saya minta maaf*
no	*tidak*	excuse me	*maafkan saya*
please	*tolong/silakan*	help!	*tolong!*
thank you	*terima kasih*	today	*hari ini*
hello	*hello/apa khabar*	tomorrow	*besok*
good morning	*selamat pagi*	yesterday	*semalam*
goodnight	*selamat malam*	open	*buka*
goodbye	*selamat tinggal*	closed	*tutup*

Acknowledgments

The Automobile Assocation wishes to thank the following photographers and libraries for their assistance in the preparation of this book:
BRUCE COLEMAN COLLECTION 65; FIONA DUNLOP 86, 87, 88, 88/9, 90; FOOTPRINTS 20/1 (Nick Hanna), 77 and 84 (P Waldock); GETTY IMAGES 14; JAMES DAVIS F/cover (b): Kuantan, Chempedak Beach; MALAYSIA TOURISM PROMOTION BOARD 9a; MARY EVANS PICTURE LIBRARY 10, 11; MRI BANKERS'S GUIDE TO FOREIGN CURRENCY 119; NATURE PHOTOGRAPHERS LTD 66a, 66b and 66c (J Sutherland); PICTOR/PHOTOBANK SINGAPORE 56; PICTURES F/cover (c): young girl; RADIN MOHD NOH SALEH 23; SPECTRUM COLOUR LIBRARY 83.

The remaining photographs are held in the Association's own library (AA PHOTO LIBRARY) and were taken by N Hanna 1, 6a, 6b, 15b, 18, 19, 22, 45, 72, 75, 78, 79; K Paterson F/cover (a): Pulau Kapas, F/cover (d); Cheong Patt Tze Masio, B/cover: cakes, 2, 5a, 7, 8a, 8b, 8c, 12/13, 15a, 16, 17, 20, 21a, 24, 27a, 27b, 28/9, 30, 31, 34, 35, 36, 37, 38, 39, 41, 42, 43, 44, 46, 47, 48, 49, 50, 51, 52, 53, 54/5, 57, 58, 59, 60, 61, 62, 63, 64, 67, 68/9, 70, 71, 73, 80, 81a, 81b, 91b, 117a, 117b.

Contributors Copy editor: Nia Williams Page Layout: The Company of Designers Verifier: Polly Phillimore Researcher (Practical Matters): Colin Follett Indexer: Marie Lorimer Updater: S L Wong

Dear Essential Traveller

Your comments, opinions and recommendations are very important to us. So please help us to improve our travel guides by taking a few minutes to complete this simple questionnaire.

You do not need a stamp (unless posted outside the UK). If you do not want to cut this page from your guide, then photocopy it or write your answers on a plain sheet of paper.

Send to: **The Editor, AA World Travel Guides, FREEPOST SCE 4598, Basingstoke RG21 4GY.**

Your recommendations...

We always encourage readers' recommendations for restaurants, nightlife or shopping – if your recommendation is used in the next edition of the guide, we will send you a *FREE* AA *Essential* **Guide** of your choice. Please state below the establishment name, location and your reasons for recommending it.

_____

_____

_____

_____

Please send me **AA *Essential*** _____

(*see list of titles inside the front cover*)

About this guide...

Which title did you buy?

AA *Essential* _____

Where did you buy it? _____

When? m m / y y

Why did you choose an AA *Essential* Guide? _____

_____

_____

_____

_____

Did this guide meet your expectations?

Exceeded ☐   Met all ☐   Met most ☐   Fell below ☐

Please give your reasons_____

_____

_____

_____

continued on next page...

Were there any aspects of this guide that you particularly liked? _____

_____

_____

_____

Is there anything we could have done better? _____

_____

_____

_____

_____

About you...

Name (*Mr/Mrs/Ms*) _____

Address _____

_____

_____ Postcode _____

Daytime tel nos _____

Which age group are you in?
Under 25 ☐ 25–34 ☐ 35–44 ☐ 45–54 ☐ 55–64 ☐ 65+ ☐

How many trips do you make a year?
Less than one ☐ One ☐ Two ☐ Three or more ☐

Are you an AA member? Yes ☐ No ☐

About your trip...

When did you book? m m / y y   When did you travel? m m / y y
How long did you stay? _____
Was it for business or leisure? _____
Did you buy any other travel guides for your trip?
If yes, which ones? _____

_____

Thank you for taking the time to complete this questionnaire. Please send
it to us as soon as possible, and remember, you do not need a stamp
(*unless posted outside the UK*).

Happy Holidays!